BLACK
AND
WHITE

STYLES OF YOUTH MINISTRY

BLACK
AND
WHITE

STYLES OF YOUTH MINISTRY

Two Congregations in America

William R. Myers

Foreword by Thomas Kochman

Introduction by Charles R. Foster

The Pilgrim Press
New York

Chapters 2 and 3 are adapted from "St. Andrew's, An Ethnographic
Description of a White Youth Ministry Mode," a paper presented at the
Association of Professors and Researchers in Religious Education
(APRRE) in Chicago, 1985.

Chapter 7 is adapted from "Grace Church, An Ethnographic Description
of a Black Youth Ministry Model," a paper presented at the Association
of Professors and Researchers in Religious Education (APRRE) in
Washington, D.C., 1986.

Chapter 9 is adopted from a research paper entitled "Educational
Models for Youth: Black and White Contexts," presented at the
biannual conference of the Society for Research in Child Development
(SRCD), Baltimore, 1987.

Library of Congress Cataloging-in-Publication Data

Myers, William, 1942-
    Black and white styles of youth ministry : two congregations in
America / William R. Myers : foreword by Thomas Kochman :
introduction by Charles R. Foster.
        p. cm.
    Includes bibliographical references.
    ISBN 0-8298-0868-X : $12.95
    1. Church work with youth–United States–Case studies. 2. Church
work with Afro-American youth–Case studies.   3. Youth–United
States–Attitudes–Case studies.   4. Afro-American youth–Attitudes–
Case studies. 5. Youth–United States–Religious life. 6. Afro-American
youth–Religious life.   7. Presbyterian Church–United States–
Membership. 8. United Church of Christ–Membership. 9. Reformed
Church–United States–Membership.   10. United churches–United
States–Membership. I. Title.
BV4447.M93   1990   90-43961
259'.23'0973–dc20   CIP

---

10 9 8 7 6 5 4 3 2 1

Printed in the United States of America

The Pilgrim Press, 475 Riverside Drive, New York, NY 10115

For Barbara Kimes Myers

– deep within us there is love –

CONTENTS

PREFACE

Critics [of curriculum] most commonly share perceptions through written criticisms, which include descriptions, interpretation, and appraisal or judgment of the educational phenomenon. The lines between data collection, analysis, and writing are blurred. Although interpretation and appraisal are discussed separately from data collection, the reader should understand that in reality the processes are not discrete.

Dorene Doerre Ross[1]

In 1984, Union Theological Seminary of Virginia funded, through the Lilly Endowment, a qualitative research project designed to uncover the components of mainline church-based youth ministry programs, chosen from middle-class denominational settings and judged to be "effective" by area ministers, church members, judicatory officials, and me. Commonalities or contrasts were to be determined between the programs. I was to discover in St. Louis and in Chicago two appropriate contexts: one black, one white.* Jack Jeffries, the youth minister at the Anglo congregation of St. Andrew's, had once taken a course with me and I was able, with his help, to visit St. Andrew's. Highly visible within the young, white, suburban, family oriented, middle-class, and growing Presbyterian (U.S.A.) congregation, the youth program in which Jack served as choir director and youth minister seemed demanding, vibrant, and sufficiently complex for any project. Intrigued with the possibility of basing the first year of my research project at St. Andrew's, I sought and received the necessary approval to do the research through the official church board of St. Andrews.

In the early fall of that year, a white student researcher named Cliff DiMascio, chosen for his interviewing skill and

---

*All names related to both case studies, including the names of both churches, have been changed.

xv

his youth ministry experience, spent a weekend with me doing semi-structured interviews with persons from St. Andrew's youth ministry program. In addition, as observer-participants, we attended St. Andrew's programs and taped extended conversations with Jack, the youth minister. Our interviews and taped field observations were transcribed and then rearranged by us into forty generalized "observations." These "observations" about St. Andrew's youth program were typed, along with snippets of the actual transcriptions, into a "working" document. Rich Wolf, a white youth minister who had been hired to critique this document (Rich ministered in a setting similar to St. Andrew's), reflected with us on the implications of our forty observations. This process enabled a set of key themes to emerge, along with additional concerns and questions.

The time spent with Rich Wolf provided an agenda for a week-long visit to St. Andrew's. During that week we revisited some of our original interviewees, sought conversations with others who initially had not been available, arranged for visits to important settings (like the high school and Southtown Mall), and generally submerged ourselves in the youths' white suburban culture. After each conversation and visit we would record what we had seen or heard. Again, this taped material was transcribed and an initial case study describing St. Andrew's youth ministry was written. This initial case study was mailed to several St. Andrew's members; Cliff and I interviewed these persons as to their reactions to this document. We then added to and edited the case study out of our new understandings. In addition, an ethnographer from the University of Illinois at Chicago, Thomas Kochman, critiqued the document and our progress. A final case study was presented to key informants who agreed that this document "caught" the meaning of what youth ministry means at St. Andrew's.

This process was repeated with Grace Church, a large and growing urban black (United Church of Christ) congregation with a powerful minister, Micah Able, who was willing to open Grace's doors for our research project. Zenobia Brooks, a black student from Chicago Theological Seminary familiar with the setting and with youth ministry, served as my Grace Church research associate. She, along with Bobby McCarroll, a black pastor interested in the process, offered clear reflections on my often confused interviews and observations. The resultant case study was read and approved by key persons at Grace Church, again with a written affirmation that this was "how it really was" regarding youth ministry at Grace Church.

A Chicago Theological Seminary "Seminar on Black and White Styles" (four black and four white students) struggled with both written descriptions and forty area ministers (twenty black, twenty white) in a one-day conference reflecting on the implications of both cases for youth ministry. At this conference two hired consultants, Rich Wolf (white) and Joyce Favors (black), offered formal critiques of Grace Church and St. Andrew's. The comments of conference participants were recorded and transcribed. In addition, papers describing both models and their educational agendas were presented to professional colleagues at appropriate conferences.* In addition, conversations and letter-exchanges were ongoing with numerous peers, and presentations were made regarding youth ministry at "Grace and St. Andrew's" with several seminary groups and classes (among these, classes at Chicago Theological, Louisville Presbyterian, and Garrett-Evangelical proved most helpful).

The final document resulting from this extensive process is *Black and White Styles of Youth Ministry: Two Congregations in America.* Using Grace Church and St. Andrew's Church as

---

*Conference presentations included: (1) "St. Andrew's, An Ethnographic Description of a White Youth Ministry Model" was given at the Association of Professors and Researchers in Religious Education (APRRE) in Chicago, 1985; (2) "Grace Church, An Ethnographic Description of a Black Youth Ministry Model" was given at APRRE in Washington, D.C., 1986; (3) "Educational Models for Youth: Black and White Contextual Agendas" was given at the Society for Research in Child Development (SRCD) in Baltimore, 1987.

two purposively selected mainstream, middle-class, accessible, and large congregations, this book attempts to describe their "styles" of youth ministry. The resulting descriptions are particular instances of youth ministry; the author assumes no other church can or should perfectly "fit" the resulting descriptions of ministry.

Current quantitative research done by Dean Hoge of Catholic University generally supports the conclusions of this book. Hoge, combining data on sixteen thousand Protestant youth from 1984 and 1985 with a one-time survey by the Search Institute of Minneapolis in 1983 of 8,165 adolescents, suggests that *black* youth are more cautious than *white* adolescents about marriage and about trusting people in general. Black adolescents also believe that religion and church are more important and have more concern for the poor than do white adolescents. Hoge also notes that while white adolescents "have more friends of the *same* race than did blacks, whose friends were more often of *both* races," there were "no differences between blacks and whites on self-esteem."[2] In capsule form, Hoge presented some "Lessons for the Church" regarding his data:

> Black youth have experienced strong church life but mixed family life, while white youth have experienced strong family life but mixed church life. This statement oversimplifies reality but may catch an important truth.
>
> Church leaders serving black youth should be encouraged by the history of strong Christian nurture among many of the youth, and they should strive to deepen this commitment and extend its benefits to family and community life. Today's black youth feel some alienation from the larger society and establishment institutions, so the church has a role in enabling them to deal effectively as Christians with the existing powers in American society . . . .
>
> White church leaders might reflect on the weaker church commitment felt by white youth; the sources behind it are difficult to identify and even more difficult to influence. Also the white youth, who feel less compassion for the poor,

might benefit from experiences providing direct contact with the poor and hungry. Whether they will feel religious motivation to undertake social witness, or at least to re-evaluate their attitudes, is uncertain, since the requisite religious motivation is not always in place. Many will have no interest, given the look-out-for-number-one mentality fashionable in the 1980s. . . .

Given the relatively weak church commitment among the white adolescents, youth ministers in white churches will of course have difficulty encouraging involvement. Much else depends on this, and it will remain a foremost challenge in years ahead.[3]

While the responsibility for the final manuscript is, of course, mine, many persons assisted in its preparation. My thanks to Jeff Francis, Jeremiah Wright, Cliff DiMascio, and Zenobia Brooks, gatekeepers and co-researchers. Helpful letters were exchanged with Perry Downs, Ella Pearson Mitchell, Wesley Black, Donald Matthews, Steve Ito, and Ed Trimmer. Rich Wolf, Joyce Favors, and Bobby McCarroll offered important critical insights out of their experiences and traditions. Sara Little encouraged me in her role as the coordinator at Union Seminary of Virginia's Lilly Endowment Youth Project. Ethnographer Tom Kochman kept me honest in my research methodology. Chicago Theological Seminary supported me with a sabbatical. Chuck Foster, Dorothy Bass, Don Browning, and Jack Seymour were supportive in their critiques. Seminar students from CM 430 (Yvonne White-Morey, Karla Oberly, Cynthia Forn, Sam Kouns, Wanda Rosatoi-Martinez, Millard Southern, Jr., Lynn Hargrove, Kathy Cheney, Linda Noonan) explored, with relish, unfamiliar territory. The forty members of our one-day conference, along with Eva Salmons, scribe, subjected both case studies to depthful examination. Becky Gregg and Marsha Thomas provided consistently excellent typing. My wife, Barbara Kimes Myers, helped in the development of the research methodology and encouraged me to believe in the value of the manuscript.

WILLIAM R. MYERS

INTRODUCTION

It is not easy to be an adolescent at the end of the twentieth century. David Elkind has observed that young people are "hurried" through childhood only to reach adolescence "all grown up" without any "place to go." A major study of high schools compares their educational experience to a shopping mall that accommodates all, but caters to a special few. The daily news records the lost futures for a vast segment of the youth population due to early pregnancies, drug addiction, crime, and poverty.[1]

The difficulties youth face in negotiating the teenage years are heightened by the confusion to be found in schools, governmental agencies, and churches over their purpose, place, and role in contemporary life. The lack of clarity and coherence in church policies and strategies reflects the depth of this confusion in the institutional agencies designed to serve youth. The confusion in the church is partly theological. It permeates the discussions over the lack of coherence among ecclesial understandings of baptism, confirmation, church membership (for Protestants), and vocation. The confusion is partly sociological. Studies indicate that young people continue to "leave the church" as a part of their quest for identity in ways that are deeply rooted in American cultural history. Unlike their parents—and to an even greater extent their grandparents—these studies indicate significant numbers will not return to the church as adults.[2] The confusion is also systemic. Denominational structures have been unable to provide the variety of leadership and programatic resources to support the range of congregational efforts to engage youth in their ministries.

Immediate sources for this confusion may be traced back through changes in the philosophy and strategies of churches toward their youth during the past thirty years. The Protestant story is illustrative. Until the 1960s most Protestants described the church's ministries with adolescents as "youth work." Adult leaders or "youth workers" supervised programs designed to develop in youth the religious and moral character and the leadership skills that congregations (and their denominations) considered necessary to equip them for the roles and responsibilities they would assume as adults in the church. This concern for the future of the church influenced the approaches of congregations toward their youth.

During the 1960s the goals and structures of "youth work" in mainline Protestant churches gave way to a new emphasis upon "youth ministry." This change, prompted by a series of ecumenical discussions within the National and World Council of Churches, espoused two interrelated assumptions—one psychological and the other theological. The first reflected the growing awareness among church leaders that during adolescence, young people increasingly refine the capacities to think and act in ways characteristic of adults. The developmental character of adolescence meant that youth could no longer be described as "the church of tomorrow." Neither could the task of church ministries for youth be seen simply as "inducting young people into the Christian fellowship and preparing them for future responsible roles" in church life. Instead they must be seen as having the ability to participate with increasing sophistication in the full range of church life and mission.[3]

A second assumption reflected a corresponding new awareness on the part of many church leaders to the lack of coherence among church practices related to baptism, church membership, confirmation, and vocation. They increasingly contended that the religious movement from baptism to confirmation or church membership paralleled personal growth in identity and faith from infant dependence to the interdependence of mature adulthood. This developmental faith journey intensified their critique of the prevailing view of youth as "preparatory members" in the church and its ministry. Instead of the old separation of youth from adults in the church, the new emphasis upon youth ministry focused upon the mutuality of adult and youth in strengthening "the common life and vocation of the Christian community."[4] Programatic emphases shifted from equipping youth for the future to the character of their experience in the present.

The institutionalization of these assumptions for "youth ministry" occurred, however, at the height of the backlash to the so-called youth movement of the period symbolized by the antiwar protests, Woodstock, long hair, beards, and beads. An exploration of the connections between denominational decisions about youth ministry between 1965 and 1975, and the attitudes of the general church population toward the rebellious features of this "youth movement," lie beyond the scope of this essay.

The corresponding creation of institutional structures to implement the programatic concerns of the new youth ministry emphases, however, did not fill the void that occurred when the various denominations dismantled the structures integral to "youth work." Professional staff positions supporting congregational and denominational efforts in behalf of youth were eliminated. People with expertise in youth work specializations moved outside the structures of the churches into parachurch organizations such as Young Life and Campus Crusade, independent religious publishing houses, and autonomous training and consultative programs directed to church constituencies. Funding for youth-centered ministries diminished. Programs and resources for training youth leaders were dismantled. Ecumenical structures for collaborative activities for denominational youth collapsed and all but disappeared. General participation of youth in church sponsored programs declined significantly.

The 1980s have been marked by the scrambling effort of many congregations and some denominational leaders to reclaim responsibility for ministries to youth. After a tenyear hiatus, congregations again seek professional leadership with expertise in youth ministry. Denominational agendas again include prominent attention to youth issues. Seminaries have resumed or expanded their course offerings in youth ministry. Several denominations are once again sponsoring regional and national conferences and training programs. And several significant books have been published to guide the development of theory and programs for youth in the church.[5]

Black and White Styles of Youth Ministry is the most recent and distinctive contribution to this expanding discussion. William Myers does not propose a theory for youth ministry, although his research leads him to several conclusions that will be important to theory development. Neither does he provide a set of guidelines for the development of youth ministry, although again, his findings provide several clues to church leaders searching for them. Instead he examines two congregations—one black and one white—with strong and active youth ministries to discover in the midst of the general confusion over youth in church what makes their efforts distinctive. These two congregations do not "represent" mainline Protestant black or white churches in the United States. Their large memberships, the size of their professional staffs, a comparative abundance of financial resources, and large numbers of youth make them atypical. And yet in Myers's analysis of their efforts, at least three themes provide insight into the future shape of youth ministry in all churches.

Congregational initiative. Despite their differences in purposes and strategies, the youth ministries of St. Andrew's and Grace share several characteristics that might function as clues to congregations seeking to strengthen their own ministries with youth whatever their size or the nature of their resources. (1) Both exist in congregations with a deep level of commitment by church leaders to young people. That commitment contributes to the visibility of youth in the public places of church life—notably worship, the extensive support of the professional staff (especially the senior minister), the prioritization of youth ministry in the distribution of financial resources, and the active encouragement of parents and other lay leaders. (2) Both congregations took the initiative and full responsibility for youth ministry. They did not wait for a denominational program for encouragement or guidance. They did not recruit outside leadership or adapt a prepackaged program. Their initiative grew out of a sharp awareness of contemporary youth needs and experience, and the belief that the efforts of the church for youth could make a difference. (3) Both congregations welcomed youth in the building and in the fellowship of the church. They created an environment of acceptance and affirmation for the presence of youth. They made youth feel "at home" in the church.

The stories of Grace and St. Andrew's proclaim the possibility for the active involvement of youth in church. In his choice of these two youth ministries, however, Myers points to the possibility that in the general confusion over youth ministry purpose and strategy, congregational self-sufficiency in initiating, supporting, and sustaining youth ministry may be crucial. If this conclusion is justified (and I am increasingly convinced it is), an important message from this study for church leaders may have to do with their lack of attention to the future of youth in those churches where congregational and pastoral commitment and resources are limited.

Contextual awareness. In *Black and White Styles of Youth Ministry*, Myers explores with his readers the mutuality of influence existing among church, family, school, and community. He examines the sources for the values and assumptions espoused in the rhetoric that congregation members use to describe their youth ministries. He traces the sources for congregational visions for their youth back into the history and cultural context of each congregation. He discovers in that effort that much of the meaning of a given youth activity tends to be more complex than the words people use to describe the activity.

The point becomes obvious in contrasting the significance of the youth choirs for these two congregations. In white suburban St. Andrew's, the youth choir exists as one program option among several. Youth choose to participate, for how long, and with what kind of commitment. The choir makes an important contribution to worship, but when people describe its real value to the church, it has to do with the meaning each young person receives from their involvement in it. At Grace the difference in meaning becomes evident in the name. Youth join the "young adult choir." While membership is optional in the choir, the choir is not optional to congregational life. Instead, the young adult choir places youth in a primary leadership role in congregational worship—the central and ordering activity of congregational life. Even though the young adult choir may have intrinsic meaning for its members, its primary meaning is found in the way it enhances the corporate life of the congregation.

These differences in perspective, Myers contends, are as much cultural and historical as they are theological. These youth ministries, in other words, reveal much about the way these two congregations perceive their relationship to their cultural context. The individualism of white suburbia permeates St. Andrew's youth ministry. The corporate emphases in African-American culture influence the shape and meaning of Grace youth ministries.

This insight indicates the importance of examining the values and commitments of youth ministry activities as common as the youth choir. It points to the paradigmatic significance of this book for church leaders. It reveals in the practices of congregational life what pastors, parents, church leaders, and youth actually believe about the place of the church in its community and historical context, and how youth ministry strategies reflect those beliefs. It links the congregation to its cultural context and illustrates the extent to which youth ministries reflect their contextual values and practices.

In effect Myers holds up a mirror to the way the reader might be engaged in youth ministry. Especially for white congregations *Black and White Styles* reveals the theological compromises and accommodations church leaders often make to develop programs that fulfill community standards for success. The story of Grace Church may similarly help to clarify why black congregations concerned with being faithful to the historic experience of African-American culture have so effectively resisted the philosophies and strategies of white church youth programs and leaders.

Multicultural perspective. *Black and White Styles of Youth Ministry* does have implications for the development of youth ministry theory. Those implications are rooted in Myers's decision to examine these two youth ministries in their historical and cultural contexts. In this regard Myers again distinguishes himself from most interpreters of youth ministry who assume that youth ministry involves the creation of environments to help young people successfully negotiate the developmental learning tasks of faith and personhood. Myers begins with the church rather than with the youth who happen to come to some congregational expression of church.

In the contrast of two youth ministries distinguished by their cultural and historical heritage, Myers challenges church leaders to examine the sources of the assumptions they bring to their own work. He moves beneath the typical identification of basic psychological, theological, educational, and even political theoretical assumptions to be found in church strategies for youth, because they do not

identify adequately the cultural biases in them. He rejects
the notion that any given cultural perspective—especially
one associated with the north European heritage of most
white Protestant churches—provides an adequate perspective for viewing youth ministry. He calls instead for a
multicultural perspective on the church's approach to
youth.

At this point several of his own emerging assumptions
begin to become clear. He affirms cultural pluralism as an
expression of the givenness of human as well as other forms
of diversity in the economy of God's created order. He
recognizes that any mode of communication or any structure that orders and directs the attempts by a group of
people to transmit values and commitments from one
generation to the next must use finite cultural forms, and
these forms will in turn influence the content of those
values and commitments. And he assumes that a multicultural perspective for youth ministry is primarily an educational or interpretive one.

His purpose is not primarily to develop ministries that
will lead to some consensus across cultures or even to
facilitate communication between cultural expressions of
faith. Instead, the educational value of a multicultural
approach becomes acute in youth ministry, because during
adolescence young people recognize with growing intensity the disparity between the gospel and its specific cultural
expressions. A multicultural perspective to youth ministry,
in other words, may help church leaders and youth develop
the ability to recognize and assess the influence of any
cultural heritage upon the faith and beliefs of people. It
may help them discover the potential for idolatry in any
cultural expression of religious commitments. And it may
liberate them to discern the power of the gospel cloaked in
those cultural forms.

The multicultural perspective that emerges from this
study is most evident in the way that Myers, a European
American, enters into and participates in the African-

American congregation he studied. His approach reflects the ancient folk wisdom that people should attempt to "wear the moccasins" of the other or to "walk a second mile" with the stranger. Grace Church hospitality invited Myers into the second mile of its "walk." In that effort he learned much about African-American culture and church life. He encountered the vitality of the Christian gospel in new ways. Perhaps more important, his encounter with Grace Church heightened his critical awareness of the ways theological and cultural assumptions shaped the youth ministry of St. Andrew's and informed his own leadership as a youth minister. That new awareness contributes to his own revisioning of youth ministry.

A multicultural perspective, in other words, involves developing a conscious appreciation of the history and artifacts of one's own culture. It involves an increasing recognition of the cultural meanings of those with different heritages. It includes the development of skills to identify, affirm, and critique the contributions of cultural values and commitments in church resources and strategies for ministry. Through these assumptions Myers directs us now toward an alternative vision for youth ministry in a pluralistic society such as that to be found in the United States.

This ethnographic study of two youth ministries, in other words, is not only a lively story. It ultimately challenges the way most churches and denominations approach their ministries to youth. In that regard *Black and White Styles of Youth Ministry* should influence the agenda and the discussions on the future of youth ministry for several years.

CHARLES R. FOSTER

PROLOGUE

YOUTH AND THE INVENTION
OF ADOLESCENCE

> It is not too much to claim that "youth" is largely a social
> construct, resulting from the gradual extension of educa-
> tion which has accompanied the specialization of an indus-
> trialized economy.
>
> Richard Osmer[1]

For me, growing up in the 1950s in the northwestern
corner of Pennsylvania meant attending a one-room school-
house with a coal stove in the center of that single room and
a sixteen-hole (eight seats per side) outhouse behind that
building. Once elected to the school board, my father
worked toward constructing a new school, and sixth grade
saw me entering that new Dempseytown elementary school
building.

Living four miles from Dempseytown meant an hour's
bus ride over dirt roads before and after school, but I
enjoyed the trip, passing my classmates' homes, several of
which were simple cement block basements with tar paper
caps instead of roofs. My Dad was a machinist at Oil Well
Supply Company, and as a nine-year-old I got to see his big
Monarch Turret Lathe and the overhead crane he operated. My friends and I were the adolescent sons and
daughters of the working class. We grew up picking apples,
"grubbing" potatoes, loading bales of hay, and hunting
wildlife in the deep woods surrounding our homes. The
opening day of deer season was our number one cultural
holiday. Companies assumed most workers would be in the
woods that day, and the local high school was effectively
closed down. One year, after a solid week's absence spent

3

hunting deer, I returned to school with a written excuse, which simply read: "Bill had buck fever." The attendance office accepted the excuse as valid. We were white, Protestant, rural and blue-collar; we were adolescents accepting the values of the dominant culture as they were passed on to us; we were coming to know *as our own* the structures and values of something called the "American Dream."

Given our pluralistic nation, growing up in the woods of Pennsylvania might appear to be a normal childhood for thousands of Americans, but it remains atypical for millions more. More to the point of this book: I was raised within the informal social contracts, ideas, customs, beliefs, and values derived from and still today strongly representing early America's Euro-centric, Reformed, white, and Enlightenment depiction of reality. While this grounding vision has itself been impacted by the unfolding events of the nineteenth and twentieth centuries, it still is centered, as Martin Marty suggests, in "theocentric transformationism"—that is, a message and an intention brought from the Netherlands, Switzerland, Scotland, Germany, and England "that a sovereign God was Lord of history and should be the center of all reflection."[2] Marty continues: "With this came the notion that this God was active in history, and had called a people to help change the natural and human environment into a sphere where God's will could be done; God's kingdom might come. The Reformed were world-remakers in God's name . . . their societal thought was theocentric."[3]

Looking back, I am aware that as an adolescent I internalized the dominant culture's individualistic, competitive, and upwardly mobile ethos. At the same time, however, from early on I heard and received the reformer's religious idea of "vocation"; I was placed upon this earth *for a reason*. But what was that reason? I had no idea. But given my culture's definition of adolescence, I was a success—my picture in the yearbook showed me hoisting the school's American flag in the early morning dawn. No matter that the picture had been posed for a one-time shot; my "identity" secure, I would enter college, get a job, marry, and "successfully" join America's white middle-class.

Adolescence

Our understanding regarding adolescence is relatively new. As recently as the early nineteenth century, upon the attainment of age seven, children in this country were expected to contribute by working for the welfare of the family. There was no "adolescence" as we have come to know it. By seven a girl was expected to weave, sew, knit, and clean house; a boy of the same age was about the doing of farm chores. Relatively permanent entrance into the work force was achieved by ages eleven or twelve. For youth, this entrance into the world of work was often synonymous with the process of leaving home. In order to collect a small income, fathers would "farm out" their sons as early as age eleven or twelve. These sons could be "bound" to work in mills, factories, farms, stores, or at particular trades for room and board. After working for an agreed upon length of time, often until age twenty-one, a son was then free to return home or enter the world of work on his own. In addition to earning some family income, by such a process the son learned a trade or occasionally completed an apprenticeship.[4]

We can say that not so very long ago, through such circumstances, children moved from brief periods of dependency within the home into relatively early semi-independent situations, often accompanied by a jarring mixture of leaving home (being relatively "free" on one's own), and being totally subordinated to one's employer.[5] Reflecting upon this unique state of semi-independence, Michael Warren has noted that young people in the early nineteenth century organized and ran a wide variety of voluntary associations by themselves. He notes that even when adult sponsors were required for legal purposes, "the groups themselves tended toward independence rather than toward adult domination."[6] In fact, until the Civil War, "adulthood" was secured by leaving home, getting married, or, in certain cases, joining a church. However, as the culture changed, so did the way we came to understand the roles youth would be permitted to play within it.

According to one cultural historian, the churches of the 1880s and 1890s were defensively motivated to form "youth societies" as shields against "the alien culture of big cities and immigrants."[7] A "common thread," in all of this change, "was hostility to precocity, to adult behavior in youth. As it acquired institutional forms, the long-standing fear of precocity changed its shape. The avoidance of precocity no longer entailed merely the removal of intellectual pressures and social stimulants from youth, but *the creation of a self-contained world in which prolonged immaturity could sustain itself.*"[8] This new "world" eventually became known as "adolescence."

Initially a word popularized by G. Stanley Hall in 1904, *adolescence* emerged in the wake of industrialization and urbanization.[9] These and other forces eventuated in the removal of youth from once familiar adult and near adult roles. Public policy decisions, like the later emergence of child labor laws and compulsory public education, greatly contributed to this process. Better birth control methods and the conscious spacing of children changed the nature of the family. Having fewer children clustered closely together meant that a certain distance began to appear between generations. Educational clubs and social institutions like 4-H, scouting, the YMCA and YWCA placed children and youth under the constant control of adults. A well-known 1949 study summarized the controls placed upon "Elmtown's youth" with these words:

> By segregating young people into special institutions, such as the school, Sunday school, and later into youth organizations such as Boy Scouts and Girl Scouts for a few hours

each week, adults apparently hope that the adolescent will be spared the shock of learning the contradictions in the culture. At the same time, they believe that these institutions are building a mysterious something variously called "citizenship," "leadership," or "character" which will keep the boy or girl from being "tempted" by the "pleasures" of adult life. Thus the youth-training institutions provided by the culture are essentially negative in their objectives, for they segregate adolescents from the real world that adults know and function in. By trying to keep the maturing child ignorant of this world of conflict and contradictions, adults think they are keeping him [sic] "pure."[10]

From this point, we can see how the church (Sunday school and denominational youth fellowships) joined with those many institutions that contributed to the eventual emergence, or the "invention," of adult-controlled adolescence.

My "special institutions" where cultural directives occurred included playing baseball (the "Little League" system), attending the Presbyterian Church (Sunday school and Westminster Youth Fellowship), camping with friends (the Explorer Post of the Boy Scouts of America), and going to the weekend "teenage" dances (Friday at the YWCA; Saturday at the YMCA). A driver's licence at age sixteen and the occasional use of my parents' car opened the door to Elvis Presley movies at the nearby drive-in theater. School was assumed to be my full-time job, and I knew no one who was my age and who worked full-time. I did know four Jews and six Roman Catholics, one of whom I had the courage to date, much to the dismay of my grandmother, who was staunch in her anti-Roman Catholic feelings and who had, I later discovered, a relative in the Ku Klux Klan.

Now, leafing through the pages of my 1960 high school yearbook (the *OILCAN*), I am struck by the fact that there were no blacks in my graduating class; in fact I am hard pressed to discover any blacks in that book. That homey, small-town, white, and Protestant image was mine—but at what cost?   Where were blacks during this country's invention of adolescence?

Locked Outside: The Conditions of Slavery

From 1700 to 1861 four hundred thousand Africans were transported to the North American colonies. They became part of an Anglo-American colonial slave society in which the practices of slaveholders and other whites continuously interacted with the beliefs and behaviors of the African Americans. To be able to live and not merely exist, these black slaves built from their past heritage a new cultural pattern of their own, in part shaping it from African traditions and in part shaping it from the demands made of them in their new context. While African Americans defined who they were over the life spans of several generations of men and women, they had to work out their new patterns of living under extremely repressive conditions.[11]

While the enslavement of Africans meant the loss of family and blood kin, slaves living under adverse conditions created new forms of the kin groupings so central to their past West African experience. In his excellent study of the black family, *The Black Family in Slavery and Freedom: 1750-1925*, Herbert G. Gutman carefully examines the available documents that demonstrate the adaptive, growing, and changing African-American culture prior to and following emancipation. Gutman shows that under the poorest of circumstances, slaves formed "distinctive domestic arrangements and kin networks that nurtured a new Afro-American culture."[12] He suggests that long-term slave marriages were the norm for this emerging slave culture; this meant that "adult slaves in long marriages were direct 'models,' making it possible to pass on *slave* conceptions of marital, familial, and kin obligation from generation to generation."[13]

Gutman's conclusions sharply resist theories about black disarray and the slaves' inability to transmit African kinship values. Gutman clearly contends that immersion in this generational process impacted and taught slave children more clearly than did contact with whites or communities of free African Americans. While not minimalizing the terrible conditions of slavery, Gutman emphasizes that African values were powerfully transmitted through slave marriages. Contrary to popular understanding, white slave owners tended, in the emerging black slave culture, to favor slave marriages. This was because stable relationships between husband and wife generally meant more children, and the production of a slave child was viewed by slaveholders as an economic fact, even if adult slaves viewed the same occasion as a social and familial fact.[14]

Children were "a primary concern of the slave community."[15] African Americans, given the repressive context of slavery, understood that a fierce parental discipline, checked by grandparents, was the only practical way to raise their children. The youngest children, under the watchful eye of older slaves who no longer worked, enjoyed relative freedom. All adults, however, joined together in the common task of teaching children, by word and deed, how to survive in what can only be described as "an extraordinarily dangerous world."[16] Slave children had to be able to exist in two worlds; they had to understand, learn, and practice behaviors appropriate to both white and black contexts. Not knowing the implications of specific actions could mean death.

While whites of comparable ages were entering various forms of employment and enjoying semi-independent conditions (noted elsewhere in this Prologue), older black slave children and unmarried young adults were raised in the expectation that they would be cut away from stable family units and sold to the highest bidders.[17] Nevertheless, African Americans retained a social, racial, and religious identity, dealing with family disruptions in ways consistent with their belief system.

In this regard, Gary B. Nash has argued that slavery was never organized efficiently or rationally to the extent that every moment of a slave's existence was controlled. There was, Nash would claim, maneuvering room; slaves would stall, retaliate when barbarisms occurred, and, most of all, were able "to convince masters and overseers that their productivity was linked to obtaining a degree of social room." These "were important parts of the process by which the 'slave community' fashioned its own culture."[18]

Though blacks honorably fought in the Civil War, emancipation brought only a second-class "freedom." In the decade following the war, Congress passed five major civil rights acts and funded the Freedman's Bureau as a way to provide ex-slaves with education and economic opportunities. Returning black soldiers, however, suffered extreme abuse, as did women and children. For example, immediately following emancipation, many former slave-owners attempted to manipulate the law so that they could forcibly indenture children. In Maryland, children who were presumably free, often were dragged before proslavery judges and placed in "apprenticeships." Local judges had the power to summon the child of any *free* black if after examination the court found it "better for the habits and comfort of the child that it should be bound as an apprentice to some white person." The law provided free black apprentices with none of the nominal protection given to white apprentices. Whites had to be taught a "trade" and "educated"; blacks had to be taught a "trade." A runaway white *could not* be sold; a runaway black *could* be sold. To entice away a white meant a twenty-dollar fine; to entice away a black meant imprisonment for at least eighteen months. If a master died, white parents had to consent to the transfer of their children to another master. Black parents had no say in such matters.

Not surprisingly, so loose a law—and especially the powers assigned to justices of the peace and orphan court judges—lent itself to widespread abuse by former slave owners.[19] Filing numerous complaints against this unfair process, parents and kin sought to protect their children by confronting judges with evidence that they could support their own children. The Maryland law was ended in 1867, but not before thousands of free black children had suffered such "apprenticeships."

When President Rutherford B. Hayes removed union troops from the south, he allowed white proslavery southerners to rewrite their state constitutions. In the last quarter of the nineteenth century, the Supreme Court killed numerous civil rights laws pertaining to blacks and "permitted southern states to establish rigid systems of segregation, which kept blacks not only impoverished but in a type of bondage reminiscent of the pre-Civil War period."[20] Reconstruction's painful lesson—brought to blacks by lynchings, rapes, Jim Crow legislation, black codes, and the Ku Klux Klan—was that freedom was still not in their own hands.[21]

With Reconstruction, some African Americans moved north. The first voluntary migration occurred around 1880 as blacks headed for Kansas, leaving the lower south and its unbearable patterns of violence. Second and third waves of migration were tied to World Wars I and II employment possibilities. By 1950 the majority of African Americans were urban. In a thirty-year span (1940-1970), almost the same number of persons (four million blacks) moved from rural areas into the cities as occurred over an entire century (1820-1920), when whites left Europe for the United States.[22] Urban unemployment often greeted those who had left the rural countryside. For the past sixty years unemployment has continued at disaster levels for blacks. A 1989 National League of Cities report notes that more than 21 percent of African Americans living in big cities were "persistently poor" throughout the ten years between 1974 and 1983, compared with the rate of less than 3 percent unemployment for nonblacks.[23]

Vocation: A Calling

While these conditions continue today, like many Anglo-Americans raised in the 1950s I had never met an African American. Understanding the plight of Africans transported two hundred years ago to these shores was not one of my high priorities. The first in our family to graduate from college, I chose to attend Westminster College because I had once gone with a church youth group to a football game for a Westminster "homecoming" celebration. In my unintentional existence, I expected that, being the best of all possible worlds, good things would naturally happen to me. But in my freshman year, I was diagnosed as "working on a stomach ulcer"; the stress of competing for grades had gotten to me. I had believed college was supposed to be uncomplicated, and in a way it was—even the Cuban missile crisis seemed to be more of an irritant than a reality. So when my fraternity chapter pushed our national organization to admit blacks, the national headquarters acquiesced, and in the wake of our local fraternity chapter's "victory," we congratulated ourselves by saying, "After all, this is America, and blacks have rights, too." We had seventy members in our fraternity chapter; one was black.

Nevertheless, the "American dream" seemed to "work," at least for me, until the death of John Kennedy. On the day Kennedy died, I was engaged in a pleasant inter-fraternity rivalry—utilizing a "Beverly Hillbilly" theme, our chapter expected to win the interfraternity "king" competition with ease. Our final day of campaigning was interrupted by the news that the president had been assassinated. The competition ended; little knots of students gathered to talk; many wept.

Kennedy's death ripped my quiet, untroubled existence into shreds. Embedded in my own little world, I had assumed life would always remain more or less the same, when suddenly the world intruded. Having planned to enter a graduate school in order to become a professor of history at some small college, I now found myself readdressing the possibility of attending seminary. Not only was my fiancée surprised at this idea; the admissions officer from the nearby seminary was also curious (Had he not regularly visited my school? Why had I not made myself known to him or attended a "seminary orientation" meeting?). My answers were vague and confused, but underneath was the certainty that the very core of who and what "I" was remained in jeopardy unless the idea of "faith" was addressed by me in depth.[24]

In 1964 I intentionally enrolled in seminary for a year's exploration of the issues of faith and culture as they impacted me. I read Niebuhr, Bonhoeffer, and Tillich. I also met with groups of concerned faculty and students who were discussing the crisis in our country over the civil rights movement. While my homespun image of America had little room for the violence of the cattle prods being used against civil rights demonstrators, I was not certain about what we could or should do. I found myself, however, being drawn to the comments of Mike Smathers, a white southerner, and Charles Marx, a black man who was deeply concerned about what was happening in the south.[25] Both felt we should go to Atlanta and help Martin Luther King Jr.

A favorite passage of mine is the one describing Jesus "walking on the water" (Matthew 14:23-33). "Walking on water" is, for me, a helpful metaphor for *transcendence*, the active process of leaving an embedded place and moving beyond the limits of an old setting. Transcendence therefore is intrinsic to being fully human.[26] It is at the core of what we describe as "praxis" or as "conscientization."[27] In the passage taken from Matthew, however, Peter, our braggart brother, assumes he can walk on the water *by himself*, and strides out, unafraid. When he slips beneath a wave, he reaches up and grabs the extended hand of Jesus, who pulls him into the boat, even as they cross over into a new relationship, a new way of being. Here "standing alone" is *transcended* into "standing with."

Never having been south before for any reason, going to Atlanta seemed very risky to me. However, as a group—a "community"—we decided in fear and trembling to journey south to assist the Southern Christian Leadership Conference (SCLC) in whatever way seemed appropriate. Looking back now, I would not want to romanticize those days or that decision—we were frightened, but we felt called to walk, *together*, onto those waters of racism, confident that Christ was already out there in front of us. Arriving in Atlanta at King's "Freedom Center," we met Hosea Williams, organized ourselves into integrated "advance teams," and scattered across the south, checking out the leaders in various counties for potential SCLC actions later that summer.[28]

While we were in the field, each night we would check in and send a single telephone call northward, reaching back home to our loved ones. Through this vehicle we quickly discovered that all was not well back home—one of the white seminarians working with us lost his field education placement when that "home" church discovered he had "gone south." We expected problems like this to surface, but we were not prepared to hear from his wife that anonymous phone callers were wishing that Jim might come home "in a casket."[29] Racism, we decided, was not only "a southern issue."

One day our team went in search of a sharecropper who was reputed to be the key black leader in an important county. Our inquiries led us to his shack at the edge of a plowed field. In that field we found an older black man who was busy working the earth with his sole possession, a worn-out red tractor. As he offered us cups of cold water from a mayonnaise jar, we talked about King and the situation in the county where the man lived. During our conversation we could see, in the distance, his mentally retarded daughter, slowly rocking on the porch in a much-repaired rocking chair. He allowed as how his girl "had some problems" from a time when "there hadn't been enough food." Our connection with King enthused this man—he was "willing to cross that river and share in that dream." He was also clear about the major issues and the potential for black leadership in his county. As we left, I turned and waved; he waved back. A proud man, standing near his red tractor, the shack he called "home," and his softly rocking child, he leaned (neverthe-less) with expectancy toward the future of his people. His name was "Hope."[30]

Youth Ministry and "Style"

Looking back I see a young, perplexed American, strug-gling with issues of faith and culture. I also recognize that I came to identify in the young, white president named John F. Kennedy and in this older, black sharecropper named Hope, two significant persons in my "cloud of witnesses," *spiritual mentors* who challenged me about how I might live and what I might do. When I returned from my brief stint with SCLC in Georgia, I knew I would be ordained and actively involved in some phase of parish ministry within this culture. But I did not live in the south; I was a northerner.

The northern church that had declared itself willing to post bond for me were I imprisoned in the south asked me to consider taking a field education seminary position with them in order to work with the youth of their community.[31] On the boundary line between a small, blue-collar town and an expanding middle-class suburban region, this was a church actively engaged in ministry *with* youth. Adults and youth staffed the weekly coffeehouse (*The Garret*), engaged in Saturday morning tutorials in the nearby housing proj-ect, co-led confirmation, served as "peer" ministers in the weekly junior high "club" (including teaching, friendly listening, and advising the monthly junior high dances), and staffed the summer work projects and the community day camps for children in grades four through six. This litany of activities centered around a lively worship experi-ence in which adolescents were welcomed and expected to play regularized, appropriate roles. My experience in this congregation and with the youth of this community laid the groundwork for my more than fifteen years as a full-time youth minister.

[handwritten marginal note: involved youth w/ worship responsibilities]

From 1965 until 1981 my calling *(vocatio)* was that of a full-time youth minister, serving in a variety of main-stream, Anglo congregations. While my concerns regarding youth ministry are contained in the book *Theological Themes of Youth Ministry*,[32] I was not equipped by those experiences, no matter how positive they were, to teach about youth ministry outside white, mainstream models. Assuming that this country is culturally homogeneous and that there is a single "correct" way to "do" youth ministry, most resources in this area are drawn from culturally ethnocentric models exclusively grounded on similar white perspectives regarding ministry. With rare exceptions, such models assume all groups, no matter how diverse, should conform to the "correct" model or be judged inadequate. Assuming America is a multicultural society, an alternative position suggests that diverse cultural ways of doing things simply are "different," neither "better" or "worse" than Anglo styles. Moreover, it is conceivable that every ethnic group can learn a great deal from such variety–that is, the church would do well to embrace the multicultural richness of this country.

Nevertheless, I am painfully aware that those blacks who sat through my initial youth ministry courses raised more issues (for me) than I had responses (for them). Such learning, however, had the advantage of being mutual, a "co-creating" kind of opportunity. A word, then, about Chicago Theological Seminary. In 1981 my vocation became that of a seminary professor at this United Church of Christ seminary next door to the University of Chicago in the heart of Chicago's southside. It is not unusual for an entering M.Div. class in this school to be half white, half black. In addition, the male/female ratio remains steady at one-to-one; more than half our students are second career folk; we have a sizeable international Ph.D. and D.Min. enrollment. We also have open cross-seminary enrollment with thirteen theological schools.

Immersion in the cultural richness of such diversity continually caused me to question and rethink what I had once considered "the" form and style of youth ministry. In contradistinction to such a limited position, given the differing cultural and historical experiences of blacks and whites in this country, it now seems reasonable for me to assert that blacks and whites have differing "styles" of youth ministry.[33]

Toward the possibility of uncovering such black and white "styles" of youth ministry, I invited several denominational leaders, church pastors, and youth ministers to nominate "good" youth ministries taking place in mainstream congregations. In this request, I offered no definition regarding the meaning of the adjective "good." From the gathered responses, Union Theological Seminary of Virginia's *Youth Ministry Project* (funded by the Lilly Endowment) agreed to support a basic research project utilizing teams of seminarians observing, interviewing, and describing two of the nominated youth ministries: "St. Andrew's"—a large, white, middle-class Presbyterian (U.S.A.) congregation; and "Grace Church"—a large, black, middle-class United Church of Christ congregation.

Once we had congregational descriptions, I asked key persons from each church to respond to the following questions: "Is this the way youth ministry actually happens at Grace Church/St. Andrew's? Is our description of this church's youth ministry a fair one? Should there be, from your perspective, additions or corrections to the descriptions we have written?" Their responses, corrections, and qualifications were then incorporated into our descriptive pictures of the youth ministries of both churches. Those descriptions were then presented at several research oriented conferences and annual meetings (see Preface for a more complete description of the research methodology). This book, however, goes beyond the purely descriptive ethnographic methodology into a critical analysis of the American religious scene, as mediated by these two cases.

Most American congregations are constituted along racial lines: St. Andrew's is the Anglo-American, or "white" church of this study, while the African-American, or "black" congregation, is embodied in Grace Church. Gayraud S. Wilmore suggests, in the American context, that "to speak of a *Black* Christianity is simply to refer to a social and cultural fact of life." He continues: "It just happens to be a fact that for the more than four hundred years of Black history in the New World, eighty-five to ninety percent of all Black Christians have worshiped with people of their own race in all-Black congregations." He concludes: "As we might expect, certain realities and characteristics of faith and life are attached to that simple fact."[34] Rather than avoiding this "simple fact," it should be possible to ascertain some of the "realities and characteristics" that can be described as composing "white and black" *styles* of youth ministry.

In *Black and White Styles in Conflict*, Thomas Kochman affirms that blacks and whites carry differing "styles" of behavior as well as "levels of spiritual intensity" into public debate: "The black mode—that of black community people—is high-keyed: animated, interpersonal, and confrontational. The white mode—that of the middle class—is relatively low-keyed; dispassionate, impersonal, and non-challenging. The first is characteristic of involvement; it is heated, loud, and generates affect. The second is characteristic of detachment and is cool, quiet, and without affect."[35] The differing "styles" of blacks and whites are often misunderstood; "whites still regard the black argumentative mode as dysfunctional because of their view that reason and emotion work against each other."[36]

In public conversation and debate, whites consider themselves to be *spokespersons*, not *advocates*. This is because whites believe that each idea should be debated on its own merits—that is, the subjective involvement and the passion attached to such personal stances has no relevance to an idea's negative or positive value. A dispassionate, impersonal, detached, and just stance is imperative for fair argumentation. Blacks, on the other hand, get involved. Kochman quotes Joan McCarty, a black teacher of black students, who states: "I've personally found it difficult in my classes to get people just to discuss an issue. They invariably take sides. Sometimes being neutral is looked upon with disdain."[37]

According to Kochman, the reason for such diversity in the black and white approaches to communication is that African-American culture "allows its members considerably greater freedom to assert and express themselves than does white culture. Black culture values individually regulated self-assertion. It also values spontaneous expression of feeling."[38]

James M. Gustafson suggests that "there can be individual and communal patterns of behavior in the world that have consistency enough to be called styles."[39] He indicates that a "style" contains both descriptive and qualitative elements—that is, while a "style of art" may describe a particular work, the artist may or may not qualitatively be affirmed as having "excellent style." According to Gustafson, various styles may coexist at the same time within any given community.[40] Thus, while we might be able to *describe* "black and white styles of youth ministry within the American mainstream denominations," for example, Gustafson's argument raises the sticky *qualitative* question—Is one style "better" than other styles? And, if one is better, should we affirm that style as *normative* for the community? Here Gustafson cautions us, noting that his concern rests with "how lives get shaped," and not with the censoring or ranking of certain "styles" of shaping. While recognizing that people "become lyre players by playing the lyre, and builders by building," Gustafson suggests "we need to explore what forms the conscience, what centers bring life to wholeness and integrity and 'style,' what brings lasting dispositions into being that give order and direction to gesture, word, and deed."[41] Gustafson asks us *to think critically as we describe the intentional processes that shape and give life to particular* "styles."

Gustafson is not alone in calling us to reflect upon "what centers bring life to wholeness and integrity and *style*."

Henry Mitchell, an African-American preacher, affirms the
need for the church to rethink what role black and white
styles might intentionally and complementarily perform in
our pluralistic society. He is aware, however, that "when
whites begin losing their young people and facing other
weaknesses in their faith, they have carefully avoided black
models in their search for answers . . . [settling] for the
narrow impoverishment of only one culture."[42] *Intentional-
ity* regarding the choice of a particular "style" of youth
ministry does not necessarily close the door on pluralism;
it only cautions the architects of a particular congregation's
model for youth ministry to be aware of the potential
consequences embodied in particular "words" and "deeds."
Certainly not *all* styles of youth ministry are necessarily
"good" for every church. In effect, using Gustafson's
words, "we need to see more clearly the style of Christian
life that helps us conform our culture and society, our time
and place, to the grace and will of God."[43]

While students and consultants (black and white) assisted me in organizing the descriptions and in "unpacking"
the implications of the congregations we observed, I am
well aware that my "insider" status as a white, onetime
suburban youth minister has enabled me to ascertain the
subtle nuances involved in the white congregation's youth
ministry. In similar fashion, because I am white, I am more
of an "observer" regarding the black congregation's understanding of youth ministry. Nevertheless, by sharing papers
at professional conferences, eliciting helpful comments
from friends, and by holding a one-day "workshop" for
twenty whites and twenty blacks on the "styles" of youth
ministry, I am led to believe that this book, while not the
final word about black and white "styles" of youth ministry,
is on the right track.[44]

I am also led, however, through the reading of an essay
by Walter Brueggemann entitled "Teaching as Witness" to
claim my own values in the writing of this book.[45] I agree
with Brueggemann's critique of "the dominant mode of

experience and perception in the West."[46] Relying on the sociological insights of Robert Bellah, the economic analysis of Crawford McPherson, and the critical philosophical reflection of Alasdair MacIntyre, Brueggemann suggests that *possessive and emotive individualism is ascendant to a crippling degree in dominant* (and here I read "white") *Western culture.* What is needed, Brueggemann suggests, is "teaching as witness."

Teaching as "witness," for Brueggemann, invites "the learner and the learning community to share in and reflect upon a particular alternative claim, to make a commitment out beyond one's self, needs, and desires to a larger public, social possibility."[47] The "larger possibility," as I see it, is for white religious educators and youth ministers (like myself) to take off our ethnocentric blinders, admit that other youth ministry models often catch and confront us in our blind spots, and to move forward into broader-visioned possibilities. As an educator, I find teaching as "witness" (to what I perceive to be "true") an important concept underlying and strengthening this book.

I recognize, however, that such a position (as "witness") undoubtedly "skews" my research. Nevertheless, I invite the reader into my journey, convinced that to the degree my journey rings "true," it will spark comparative responses out of the reader's personal experiences.[48] Anchored by historical analysis, ethnographic description, and a critical position as "witness" regarding "dominant culture," I believe the following chapters begin to uncover the implications of black and white "styles" of youth ministry in today's American congregations.

PART
ONE

YOUTH MINISTRY AND THE
CONFIRMATION OF
CULTURE

Chapters 1 through 4 describe youth ministry as it occurs at St. Andrew's, a large, white, middle-class, Presbyterian (U.S.A.) congregation located in the suburban midwest.

While no two Anglo-American congregations are exactly alike, St. Andrew's enjoys the reputation of being a consistently solid example of what "good" youth ministry looks like in a white, mainstream, denominational congregation.

Later chapters (9 and 10) sharply focus on how St. Andrew's illustrates the promise and the problems of "white style" youth ministry. Chapter 1 ("St. Andrew's: A White Context") and chapter 2 ("Uneasy in Eden") are primarily descriptive accounts regarding St. Andrew's youth ministry, while chapter 3 ("Double Vision: Program Director or Ritual Elder?") and chapter 4 ("Embracing Dominant Culture") pose two contextual dilemmas always facing those leaders and participants involved in "white style" youth ministry.

Through such description and analysis, chapters 1 through 4 suggest that "white style" youth ministries (like St. Andrew's) have perhaps too easily accommodated themselves to dominant American culture, resulting in an inability to critically reflect upon the alternative religious roles open to a faith community within that culture.

By its tacit acceptance of America's dominant cultural ethos, the youth ministry program of a church like St. Andrew's tends to serve as a religious confirmation program for the values of the dominant American culture.

23

CHAPTER
ONE

ST. ANDREW'S:
A WHITE CONTEXT

Associate Pastor: We have some troubled youth . . . kids who just don't "fit in."

Interviewer: What do you think should happen with some of these "troubled" youth?

Associate Pastor: I've been thinking about my invitation to a group of young people . . . to begin working with them on some things that are really bothering them. Yeah, because we've got some now who have some major needs. But we don't have anybody and the youth minister can't do it cause he can't be all things to all people and he wouldn't want to be all things to all people. If I were to do it I would have to find a way to get rid of some other stuff and try to reach out to a group that really needs that strength right now before it's too late . . . Whatever the reason is . . . these are the kinds of things you do to have a full ministry with youth and we keep wanting more programs—but we're programed to death.

tape 8, p. 6.

Sitting on a hill, nestled among trees and a sizable parking lot, St. Andrew's's six-sided sanctuary resembles a circus tent being drawn up into the sky by the invisible hand of God. Thin slits of flowing stained glass compliment a circular interior worship space containing a raised baptistery, an openly-placed communion table with a chest-high pulpit on one side and five banks of choir chairs against the opposite brick wall. Blue cushions and carpet soften

contemporary pew lines. Black wrought-iron lighting fix-
tures hang from a high-arching, wooden roof.

The hallway adjacent to the main sanctuary entryway is
lined with announcements contained in metal stand-up
holders. Each announcement is lettered on one side of a
piece of cardboard, so that once the event is finished the
announcement card can be reversed and reused. Collection bins are strategically located for clothing, canned
foods, and used eyeglasses. Bulletin boards containing
pictures of new members, articles about church members
from local newspapers, and letters concerning a variety of
issues line the walls. Printed material from the church is
located in abundance on a small table near the midpoint of
this hallway. People entering the sanctuary pass through
this hallway into a small library (which, on busy Sundays,
serves as an overflow room with folding chairs). Greeters
say "Hello" and pass people on to the ushers who escort
them to seats while providing them with bulletins to follow
the order of worship. Everyone wears a dress or suit. While
some who have entered are children (I can see a father
sitting with his arms around two children; toward the back
of my section is a cluster of five other children), the
dominant sense is that of a room filled with three hundred
white adults between thirty and forty years of age (I note
only two gray-haired folk in the pews near me). This
appears to be a young, energetic, fast-growing (fifty to
seventy-five new additions yearly) congregation.

An announcement in the bulletin indicates that today's
communion is "open to all" and includes specific words to
the effect that children can participate in the sacrament
according to each family's wishes. Communion this morning includes bread baked by the pastor's wife and grape
juice made from grapes grown behind the church building.
Banked by numerous loaves with top crusts evenly diced
into small tear-away servings, a large clay chalice filled with
grape juice rests upon the communion table.

All very traditional setting

A closer glance at the bulletin finds eight pages evenly divided between "worship" and "announcements." By count, seventy separate announcements include things like the mother-daughter banquet, pizza sales, bake sales, friends and fellowship roller skating trips, cub scout pack meetings, spinnakers evening outing, Irish dinners, Kerygma Bible Study times, proclamation choir practices, volleyball games, prayer group gatherings, property committee, and youth committee meetings. One announcement reads: "Nanny needed by Connecticut family in New York City area around May 1 or thereafter. This will be a fine opportunity for a young lady who would like to live with a good family in the East. If interested, call Mrs. Janusen for details." The final page of the bulletin issues a welcome and an invitation to the work of St. Andrew's with these words:

> Welcome to St. Andrew's Church. We hope you find this worship service meaningful. We invite you to return soon and participate in the fuller program of the church. St. Andrew's is endeavoring to live as a responsible community of believers. We welcome you to work. Please join us in the Great Hall following worship, so that we may greet you personally at our Welcome Center.

My reading of the bulletin has been accompanied by music from a youth bell choir and the pipe organ, but I refocus as the library entrance to the sanctuary fills with blue-robed choir members. Having sung three lines, the choir pauses as a single adult voice is raised in a "call to worship," and all break into the hymn, "Praise my Soul, The King of Heaven." Two ministers, clothed in black robes, enter the sanctuary trailing the choir's procession. The bulletin's listing of the senior pastor as "Dr." finds confirmation in one man's doctoral stripes. An associate, also male, wears an academic robe and is listed in the bulletin as "Mr."

As we all stand, the associate pastor leads in prayers of adoration and confession:

> Lord God, pardon all that we have done in willful or
> thoughtless disregard of your honor and of our neighbor's
> good. If we have this day by word or deed made life harder
> for any of our brothers or sisters, or made faith in your
> goodness less easy, forgive us, Gracious Father, Amen.

This "confession" is followed by a verbal "assurance of pardon" led by the associate and ending with, "In Christ's name, our sins are forgiven, Amen." A "seating interlude" follows the congregation's singing of "The Gloria Patri." Then the choir, fifty strong, sings in black dialect the anthem, "Soon All Will Be Done," by William L. Dawson.

A guest from a school for native Americans speaks about that school's mission. "Offertory sentences for the pastoral prayer" elicits an older woman's comment about a safe escape from a near accident (I am later told she regularly has contributions during this slot). Chuckles from the congregation greet her statement, but the senior pastor deals gently with her concern and then moves into the pastoral prayer. This prayer ends; an anthem is sung, and the offering is collected, brought forward, and removed during the congregation's singing of the doxology. Having stood to sing the doxology, the congregation now sits to hear the sermon. Rising in the pulpit, the tall, black-robed senior pastor continues his series on "Visiting the Prophets" with a retelling of Hosea. A manuscript is used and the delivery is evenly modulated and paced. God's forgiveness is emphasized for the "harlot" and for Israel; contemporary application is left to the listener. The pastor's goal, in his words, is to "tell a story that enlightens" (tape 20, p. 18).

As the sermon ends, the pastor asks the congregation to rise and reaffirm their faith. This is done using these words:

> The one sufficient revelation of God is Jesus Christ, the
> word of God Incarnate, about whom the Holy Scriptures,
> which are received and obeyed as the Word of God, have
> been written. The Scriptures are not a witness among
> others, but the witness without parallel. The church has
> received the books of the Old and New Testaments as

prophetic and apostolic testimony, in which it hears the
word of God, and by which its faith and obedience are
nourished and regulated.

The associate introduces "The Sacrament of the Lord's
Supper." In this introduction there is no blessing, elevation,
pouring, or breaking of the elements. The "invitation" is
given from a small book held by the associate, from which
he reads. "Amazing Grace" is sung and the deacons,
including one youth (who is the senior pastor's son), several
women, and a larger number of men approach the communion table to receive, in unison, the evenly diced loaves
of bread. Carrying each loaf to designated rows, these
deacons stand by as members of the congregation tear off
the small, diced sections of precut bread, holding them in
order that all might eat in unison. The bulletin notes: "With
each of the elements, you are asked to hold them until all
have been served. We will then partake together." Leftover
pieces of bread are returned to the table; the deacons are
seated and served; the pastors are served by the deacons; all
eat. The same procedure occurs with the grape juice. In
unison, the congregation prays:

> Almighty and everliving God, we most heartily thank you
> that in your great love you have fed us at your table with this
> spiritual food, and have assured us of your goodness
> toward us. And we pray now, O Heavenly Father, to assist
> us with your grace that we may continue in this holy
> fellowship, and live to your glory; through Jesus Christ our
> Lord; Amen.

A final hymn is sung, the benediction is given, and people
move toward the library entryway where the senior minister
and his wife stand, the minister greeting participants, the
wife collecting messages and notes given to the minister by
worshipers. These messages will be responded to during
the week.

Three worship services will be held this morning. After
each service several families carrying little baskets lined

with plastic collect communion cups. Children seven or
eight years old pull used bulletins out of the hymnbook
racks. Several such teams ready the sanctuary for the next
cluster of worshipers.

Coffee and doughnuts are available after the service in
the Great Hall. Junior highs raise money by running a
donation table filled with doughnuts and coffee selections.
The money earned from this continuous project, as with
their paper recycling project, will go to a fully paid, summer
amusement park visit.

The Setting: Crest is Best

Lying due north of a large midwestern city in the middle
of Armstrong County, the area defined as "Crestwood" is
surrounded by other middle-class suburbs. Considered the
city's "prime area" for suburban dwelling, Crestwood is at
or near the top of such indexes:

> Educationally and occupationally, the congregation of St.
> Andrew's does not vary significantly from that of the com-
> munity. Members are in professions, management, teach-
> ing and school administration, sales, engineering and full-
> time homemaking. A large number have college degrees
> and many have graduate degrees. Most live within a five-
> mile radius of the church. [*Church Profile*, 1981]

The 1980 census indicates the median age of Crestwood to
be thirty-two years of age.

At the quarter-century mark, the church of St. Andrew's
continues to grow. When questioned as to why, people
point toward the church's ability to provide programs for
an increasing number of young families. With three
hundred members added since the last building campaign,
talk has now turned to space and personnel needs for the
next fifteen years. Currently the three ministers conduct
three Sunday worship services, but an expansion to four

services seems likely. The associate minister comments on what might happen:

> We could add 300 more in the next five years, which could very well happen. You know, I don't see anything right now that's going to shut back the flood gate. There's no other church making plans; the other churches around here are not doing anything different that's going to start bringing all these new people to them; construction is still booming; condos are going up all over the place; also, they are adding a lot of single family homes. The planning council doesn't plan to do anything out here to slow down the building, other than going to like an acre and a half or something like that per individual house because of the lack of sewer systems that they're not going to put in; but, other than that, the people are where the homes are going in, and there's no St. Andrew's church out there. So another 300 members in another five or six years, there's 1,550. Three worship services, right now we're at 550 to 600 on Sunday with three worship services, and the early one doesn't attract too many yet, maybe 60, 70, 80 at the most. Even if we had a balance, say 300 at all three of those services, we'd be seated two-thirds of the way back in the library, so we'll have to go to four worship services. [tape 16, pp. 18-19]

Along with this fourth worship service and some added space would come a fourth associate minister for congregational care, primarily defined as someone hired to do counseling and calling, particularly with young families. In the words of one adult church member: "This church is a power base, given the people that are here. This is a community where there are children and where there will continue to be children . . . This is not an aging community . . . we have a lot of youth coming up" (tape 2, pp. 27-28). In fact, more than a third of the church families include teenagers (1981 *Church Profile*), and 95 percent of these youth attend Crestwood High School (*Crest*). The remaining 5 percent are from Jamesen High School. The dominance of Crest is at once positive and negative. Crest is a competitive, tough school. Their motto, "Crest is Best,"

lays it on the line. A parent comments: "The school is a little
snobbish. Let me emphasize it's an excellent school, but
they're good and they know it. Their slogan, after all, is
'Crest is Best'! So, you know, that kind of says it all. They're
good young people, but I think they have a tendency to have
a little bit of, you know, snobbishness about them" (tape 1,
p. 3).

Jamesen, the school from the northern edge bordering
Armstrong County, often draws the derisive slogan, "man-
sions and manure." Only a few years ago the land surrounding Jamesen was farmland. Today large new homes edge
outward. Because of the rural aspect, still dominant, Jamesen
is smaller, less intense, more friendly. One mother re-
marked: "It's a much more friendly school than Crest is
because there's a lot of good old farm kids who go there. My
sons have had friends who've gotten up at four in the
morning to milk the cows and take care of the animals before
they come to school. You would not find that at Crest" (tape
1, p. 3). Crest revels in accumulating merit scholars and
athletic trophies. The school's public slant is toward com-
petitiveness. The agenda is "success." And everyone agrees,
Crest is best:

> I walked into Crest and immediately saw the trophy cases,
> but even before the trophy cases are the honor rolls on the
> left side. To the immediate left you see the highest honor
> roll, the high honor roll, and then the regular honor roll, and
> all the cute trophies and all that stuff. There are trophies all
> over the school, in the library, on top of the shelves; almost
> in every hallway there seems to be trophies [tape 15, p. 1]

Crest High School is a dominant reason many adults
choose to settle in Crestwood. Indeed, the "Crest is best"
base has negated, over the years, participation at St. Andrew's by those youth whose parents live to the north (and
Jamesen) but who choose to attend St. Andrew's. For
example, one mother complains, "A negative attitude still
exists because my boys are not all that old and never, being

from Jamesen, they never were involved in the youth programs here" (tape 1, p. 6). Competitive success through the Crest (not the Jamesen) system is perceived by parents and by youth to be the gateway to America's "good life."

Cultural Expectations

Crestwood is a stop on the American ladder of success. Kids raised here are "good kids," polite, educated, obedient, competitive products of well-heeled, middle-and upper-middle-class professional families. Ninety percent of those graduating from Crestwood High School are expected to and will attend college. The cultural system, predominantly white, professional, youth-and family-centered, appears to be working for those adults who have arrived at Crestwood. Active participants in what appears to be a satisfactory process, adults living in Crestwood look comfortable; cultural and personal values seem congruent; they appear to have "arrived."

Observations from the places youth gather (Southtown Mall, McDonald's, Teen Center, etc.) as well as at St. Andrew's confirm that youth from this area are clean-cut, expensively dressed, and polite. Conversations with youth in Southtown Mall are friendly and spontaneous. McDonald's police security personnel do not have to be anything other than low-key and gentle; conversations among youth, even on a Friday, are never beyond a certain norm; and when a police officer indicates someone should move on, that youth complies with courtesy.

Socially adept, presenting themselves appropriately and politely at every occasion, even the haircuts of these youth fit well within adult standards. Spoken language is error-free. Teeth have been realigned into near perfect smiles. Healthy specimens, they practice their "good kid" image with friends in school, at Southtown Mall, or McDonald's. The mall's "marble park" provides younger and older youth with a place for exploring social interactions and the consumer world. Movies and music are powerful ingredients of this mixture. When youth find access to automobiles they move out—frequently "to party" with alcohol. Having taken one step out of the home, these youth gravitate back to McDonald's, the place of parental choice for toddlers and elementary school children. Now "grownup," older youth enter McDonald's on their own terms every Friday night to see and be seen. Again, police confirm, these are "good kids"; maybe "spoiled" a bit, but "good kids." They obey the rules. ←or at least appear this way

Some adults at St. Andrew's question this vision. The youth committee chairperson wants to see youth "become a little bit more involved and aware that everyone is not white, affluent, and in the same situation as St. Andrew's youth are. I think our young people out here are extremely naive as to what is going on in the real world. Really, just the Senior High Fellowship has been doing this kind of exposure" (tape 1, pp. 14-15). She would like the youth to have more exposure to a variety of kinds of persons: "Not everyone has it as easily as these kids do. They really want for nothing and we as parents all agree that we've probably given them far too much in material things and also in terms of ample opportunities. Things are just too readily available for them. It's like whatever you want to do—it's OK, you do it" (tape 1, p. 15).

But adults and youth who live in Crestwood, and who challenge this suburban culture and its particular value system, face a difficult dilemma. Crest High School dominates and structures a youth's time. To live in Crestwood and attend Crest High School means either (1) accepting, in large part, the Crest system, (2) negotiating a place to stand within, but not of the system, or of (3) rejecting the system and moving, in some sense, outside it. Crest's principal, Mr. Cardinal, puts it like this:

> It's a big school and it's full of responsibility and freedom. Responsibility means that you have consequences for ac-

tions but freedom means that we don't have any rule books
or any kinds of guidelines in terms of what you can wear or
what you can't wear or what cut policy is or anything like
that. We have no information on that; instead, as you come
in the door we assume that we can trust you unless you
prove otherwise, and that if you go ahead with that, our
hope is that you fly; but, there is also a sizeable drop if you
don't plug into the system. Sometime things get to a point
that's beyond the capacity of the school to do anything
other than to simply say, "Well, you should go to a private
school or go to, in other words, a different kind of situation." The advantage is if you fit the structure, you have
total freedom in some sense; do whatever you want to do.
If you don't fit the structure, you won't really be aware until
it gets to a point where it may be crippling for you; and, in
terms of expectations here, we'll have to give you the boot.
[tape 17, p. 26]

And youth with a long way to fall, fall hard. Those who work
with youth through Crestwood's social agencies indicate
that not all youth readily fit into the "Crest is best" system.
Some are victims of poor parenting, abuse, and abandonment. Still others have discovered alternative salvation
agents. One strung-out young man, high on drugs, greeted
us from his perch on a Crestwood High School radiator,
almost falling onto the floor in the process. Decidedly out
of step with the system, he told us how, when everything
gets to be "too much," he illegally climbs the tallest water
tank in Armstrong county and sits through the night,
"above it all," until the sun rises once again (tape 5, p. 10).

One of the best attended adult forums held at St.
Andrew's deals with stress management. Sixty to eighty
adults regularly attend this forum with a sizable number
electing to engage in six additional one-night-per-week
sessions. The associate minister in charge notes that most
of the participants come from homes where youth are
present. He states:

That doesn't mean that the teens are creating the stress, but
it does mean that these parents are at a period in their lives

where they can see nothing but stress for themselves. They are in their late thirties, early forties; they're the ones under the most stress because all of these people (with very few exceptions, like all of the men, I believe) are in their upward point; in their late thirties or early forties; and if they're not rising in their career at that age it's a problem. As far as they're concerned nothing is as important as the business world—work, work; it carries over into church, i.e., St. Andrew's church, I mean, no doubt about it. Probably 80 percent of the adult males are in some sort of sales management, or engineering, or positions closely related to business; we've got a lot of engineers. There is a lot of stress. [tape 16, p. 16]

Stress means some things happen that involve police and the court system. Charged with the intake of adolescent first offenders, one of the deputies of Armstrong County's court system states that of the cases she deals with, most have to do with parents who want to dump their adolescents (tape 18, p. 10). In order to do this, many of the parents hire "high-priced attorneys to do it for them" (tape 18, p. 12). These parents want the court to declare their adolescents incorrigible and take over parental responsibilities for raising the children. The St. Andrew's senior minister puts it like this:

There's an interesting mix out there, um, you've got some families who are just as responsible and caring and dedicated to healthy parenthood, healthy children, healthy family life in the best way possible, and you also have folks who really have a need to achieve and win financially and all the status stuff that can go with that, such that, you know, you feel sometimes like the kids are ... well, an impediment to that goal. They take a certain amount of time and resources and energy and all that so ... they decide to dump the kids. [tape 20, p. 3]

CHAPTER
TWO

UNEASY IN EDEN

Interviewer: What's Southtown Mall all about anyway?

Jason (a senior high): It's mostly video games, clothing shops and stuff like that, all indoors with lots of places. It's impossible to get around on Saturdays in there, probably 50 percent kids, mostly just hanging out.

Interviewer: How long would someone hang out if they went over there . . . for the afternoon? The morning? All day?

Jason: I used to go over there a lot . . . not much anymore . . . I don't have a reason to go there, but you usually hang out for three or four hours. Play around a couple of hours or looking through all the shops, the video games, eat something up there, just to say you did something, maybe see a movie, and then go home. Usually four hours is about the average hang-out time.

Interviewer: So this is a place where people congregate because they don't have anyplace to go and this has got some interesting things to do?

Jason: That's about it.

tape 11, p. 3.

A visit on a Friday night confirms that many youth are dropped at the mall an hour and a half before movie time, while others come later with their parents and simply go their separate ways to later reconnect at prearranged spots. Jack, the youth minister, suggests:

> It's like having a big playground area where parents and
> their families would come; the parents spread out the
> picnic lunch and the kids go off and play. It's a contained
> area. It has a lot of neat things to do and parents say, "This
> is okay, we're gonna go our way, you all run off and play."
> So mom and dad go off and buy a shirt, or a pair of shoes,
> or have a cup of coffee somewhere and the three kids from
> the neighborhood plus their kid make the rounds down the
> escalator, buy an ice cream cone, come up the backside,
> come through the mall like they're exploring . . . like going
> through a park and exploring the caverns, climbing the
> trees, looking at the foliage, seeing what animals are here,
> that whole bit. You know it is a . . . what can we call it . . .
> "a marble park" [tape 21A, p. 23]

The crowd visiting the mall changed about 9 P.M., but
the balance of those who stayed were junior highs. In dress
and manners, "Southtown Mall looked most like a mirror
reflection of the population living within the area. It didn't
look dangerous. It looked like a place where a kid might
spend two hours waiting for a movie. Except—it's not
waiting. It's two hours being adventurous with your friends"
(tape 21A, p. 25). During the day youth like Jason "hang
out" in this marble park. But many parents fear that
Southtown Mall is a dangerous place for junior highs to
congregate. While part of the concern centers on their lack
of control over what "might happen," as in "my kid could
get physically hurt" (tape 19, p. 8), an angry security guard
dismisses the potential danger. He feels used, as if he'd
been hired to take care of criminals and instead "got stuck
baby-sitting 6th and 7th graders" who persist "in stealing
candy bars" (tape 21A, p. 24).

A stronger concern focuses upon the mall as a cultural
consumer training program. One mother put it this way:
"This area is very materialistic. And to try and combat that
out here is just almost impossible" (tape 9, p. 12). Another
adult calls this struggle with the culture "the forever battle"
(tape 1, p. 15). Still another parent watched an adolescent
friend of the family receive the gift of a "small" Porsche. She
exclaims: "No way! You know, these things blow my mind.

That's not good for my kids. I don't think that's good for their kids but it's not good for my kids either to see all of that. I don't like that" (tape 1, p. 16). Southtown Mall seems, to these concerned parents, to be an attractive purveyor of "all of the values you would like to get rid of and push out the door; that's what Southtown Mall is and that's where these junior high kids go, and I don't like it" (tape 6, p. 21).

Teen Center, a Friday evening church-sponsored youth program, is as much a reaction to the mall as it is a conscious form of youth ministry. Still, the senior minister names it as "a ministry to youth to provide a healthy outlet in a somewhat protected environment" (tape 21, p. 18). The current chairperson of the Teen Center board sees it as one of the two options presented to Crestwood's junior highs—either Teen Center or Southtown Mall. She continues: "It's really sad that Teen Center shuts down in the summer, and that's why I keep thinking we should keep Teen Center open all summer. After all, we are air-conditioned" (tape 6, p. 21).

Teen Center was created by the laity; it was not initiated or even contemplated by the professional staff of St. Andrew's. The associate pastor remembers how, at an open examination of the then current youth program, a sizable number of parents were determined to start some kind of teen center on Friday evenings for junior highs: "I mean they knew that's what they wanted. They needed it and they were clear and within a couple of weeks, it was done. But then a lot of it goes back to the kind of homes these children come from, very goal-oriented. These parents see something they want, they jump on it, they develop it. Most everyone has the background, the necessary management skills" (tape 9, p. 16). The 1983 St. Andrew's *Annual Report* states:

> Teen Center is in its third year of existence at St. Andrew's.
> It is held on the second and fourth Friday nights of each
> month throughout the school year. It is a place for youth in

the 7th, 8th, and 9th grades to go to talk, dance, and play games. Attendance continues to grow. This year we are averaging 170 teens! There is no charge to attend Teen Center. Our expenses are covered by the sale of refreshments, so Teen Center continues to be a self-supporting organization. The Teen Center is guided by a board of eight adult couples and six teen representatives, and supported by volunteer chaperons. [*Annual Report*, 1983, p. 16]

Teen Center's stream of cars deposit junior highs at St. Andrew's main door, there to be met by two friendly father/chaperons. They direct all visitors to an inside membership table. Initiated in 1985, the "new" membership plan encourages "family" ownership of Teen Center and secures chaperons from the membership list. What constitutes membership in Teen Center is the act of turning in an application upon which the junior high has written his or her parent's name, phone number, and pediatrician's number, as well as the name of the hospital that he or she would like to be taken to in case of an emergency. An incentive to be a member is that since 1985 members are asked to start paying 50 cents to enter, while nonmembers are charged $1.00.

Inside the Great Hall 35 junior highs shoot basketballs at three suspended hoops in one end. Ping-pong and table games are set up at the other end near the food counter. Food can be purchased and eaten at several tables. Very few youth are seated; many eat pretzels or pizza slices while walking and talking with friends. A second sizable room has doors opened to the Great Hall. Here resides the disk jockey from the local YMCA. A line of chairs separates his turntables and speakers from the crowd of eighty to a hundred continuously dancing junior highs. The speaker volume is up as he spins the current hits. "Some of the adult chaperons shudder, you know, but we say, 'That's all right, you'll survive'" (tape 1, p. 11).

Another enclosed room is set up with television or video games. An advisor says: "It's a nice room and sometimes we have groups of girls sitting in there talking, and every once in a while you might see a couple in there with the door closed, and you go in and you say, 'How are things going?' But it's no big deal" (tape 6, p. 20). Chaperons are visible, but restrained. More than half of the chaperons come from St. Andrew's, but membership entails having at least one parent willing to chaperon, and many parents outside the church readily respond. Teen Center, as one parent suggests, "helps the parents. We get to see lots of 'community' going on, not just with the kids, but with the parents, and then with the parents and the other kids. I see my daughter's friends at Teen Center, and I see an entirely different child than I see when they are over at my house. And it's good things that we see" (tape 6, p. 17). The same parent continues: "Some of the kids are surprised at doing this in church. They say, 'In a church, I can't believe it. . . . In a church we get to do this?' It's like, 'We're having fun!' And they think it shouldn't be allowed. And I want to say, 'This is where it should happen'" (tape 6, pp. 14-15).

If someone creates a hassle at Teen Center, the advisors deal with it on the spot. If it concerns property, the church property committee gets involved. The event, in the youth committee chairperson's words, is "well-organized" (tape 1, p. 12). The rules are firm:

> They state exactly how you're to behave and the time you come and the time you leave . . . no alcohol, no drugs, no cigarettes. You come, you stay the whole evening, and you don't use the phone. When it's over, the men chaperons move outside to make sure the kids are getting in the cars and not dashing off through the neighborhoods and things like that. A lot of these kids live in the immediate subdivision, and we don't want Teen Center being out and fifty kids, you know, terrorizing the neighborhood. We want them to be picked up by parents in cars. [tape 1, pp. 12-13]

Rarely are there problems at Teen Center. One evening a woman chaperon was approached by one of the male chaperons who was concerned about some extended activity in the girl's rest room. The woman chaperon reports:

He said, "Would you please go into the girl's rest room; there are two girls in there and they've been in there a long, long time, and I'm really suspicious."

So I just trotted on in, used the rest room facilities, came on back out, and I was hysterical. I said, "Do you know what they're doing in there?"

He said, "No, what?"

I said, "They've got two curling irons plugged in, and they're doing each other's hair." They kept a curling iron hot in there, because they would be running around and dancing and oh, it gets hot, and they get sweaty and their hair falls, and they run in and they put a few curls in, and they run back out. I thought it was so funny. So we had a good laugh over it. [tape 1, p. 12]

Part of what makes Teen Center run smoothly is Teen Center's board.

[This board] is made up of an equal number of adults and young people. The youth aren't threatened, nor are the adults. Each see each other regularly at the Teen Center, and they just have kind of a common interest, and it's not like, oh, she's somebody's mom; you know, you're just kind of in it all together. And the young people have been very good about speaking out about what they like and what they don't like and things like that. So it has worked very good. [tape 1, p. 14]

Overall, the junior highs who attend Teen Center are characterized as "really good kids" (tape 6, p. 16). One church elder sums it up with these words: "From what I gather they really watch the kids and patrol the grounds. I've always felt very secure about letting kids come up here because I feel like they're all watched" (tape 12, p. 12).

Most of St. Andrew's older senior highs don't go to Southtown Mall on Friday nights anymore. They've done that for several years, "And I think they want to go someplace where it's happening, and McDonald's is the place where it's happening; and they have the wheels to get there" (tape 21B, p. 18).

McDonald's: Out of the Nest

Located in the middle of the black asphalt parking lot of a sizable shopping center, McDonald's at 10:30 on a Friday night is packed with senior highs. We enter. Several youth regard us with suspicious looks, like "Why are you here? Are you a narc?" (tape 21B, pp. 4-5). We sit at an empty booth in the middle of a crowded section, surrounded by a little "demilitarized zone" of table space that has opened up around our "adult" presence (tape 21B, p. 5).

Three police maintain order inside with a relatively light touch. When a group sits too long or is too noisy, one of the police simply says, "It's time to go." Sometimes the order is nonverbal: a finger is pointed at a youth, then pointed at the door. And that's it. No physical contact. The youth leaves without comment.

The manager is asked, "Is it always this crowded?" And he responds, "Every Friday night." And I ask, "Do they buy anything?" And he says, "Maybe they get a drink for the girl, but that's about it, except maybe once in a while somebody buys some french fries" (tape 21B, p. 7). One group explains why they are here: "We just came from the party. It got busted, and most of the people here are coming from different parties, so we're here, too. We'll go home, after. This is it. This is where everybody winds up. Everybody's here, you know" (tape 21B, p. 5).

Early in the evening everyone who entered seemed straight—that is, not on drugs. As the evening wore on, some of the arriving groups are visibly "messed up"—that is, tipsy, or on something illegal. Still, no one is really "out-of-control." A senior from the church comes over to us and addresses Jack, the youth minister, politely. The senior confirms that he just arrived from a party and that he has hopes of meeting some friends here and then going home. When he leaves, Jack notes, "He's a good kid. He's a solid kid. You're talking about an honor student. You're talking about he'll probably graduate with a four-point grade average after lettering in football every year" (tape 21B, p. 6). Jack suggests:

> This is a place where they can socialize so that they aren't out of touch, and they can still feel that they are with their friends between Friday afternoon and Monday morning. It's also a practice round for these high school juniors and seniors. They have cars. Soon they'll be on their own. Once their parents took them to McDonald's for lunch; now they go on their own terms. It's exciting, but it's safe. It's a half-step out of the door. For most, the next step is college. But tonight, after McDonald's, they go home. [tape 19, pp. 6-7]

Outside, cars are pulled together in different clusters. One group of trucks and four-wheel drive vehicles are about fifty yards from the building with youth gathered around listening to country music. Occasionally two girls break into an impromptu dance. Two sets of speakers rest on the hood of a Cherokee 4-wheel drive, sound cranked up high. Closer to the take-out window, several sizable young men in blue leather football letter jackets seem to be contemplating picking up and moving a small import car. Laughter permeates their discussion.

Bringing Them Along

Some concern is voiced by parents over the church's impact on this McDonald's crowd. Those who like Teen Center raise the possibility of something like a Senior High Teen Center: "The big activity in this area is parties that involve booze and drugs. It's primarily beer. So the game gets over, and where do you go? Why can't the church be an alternative?" (tape 10, pp. 8-9). Other than weekend "party-time," however, the church already offers this age a whole set of programs.

"Confirmation/Commissioning" class is the Great Hall Sunday morning program that ninth graders must take in order to join St. Andrew's. This is the key program for those parents who want their children to join the church. As such it is the central program of St. Andrew's youth ministry effort. This program is a kind of litmus test for parents in that, as the senior minister puts it, "Here is where you get some comprehensive idea of the parents' sense of commitment" (tape 21, p. 21). Parents who themselves do not regularly attend church will go out of their way to make certain their children join St. Andrew's. Again, the senior minister suggests that this class is strongly "related to this business of pulling in the families that haven't been to church in five years, ten years, whatever. So we'll get a lot of kids in this class who have had very spotty experience with Sunday church school, whatever, occasionally some with almost none, so this class is a concerted effort to try to bring them along" (tape 21, p. 21).

The "postcommissioning" class is the Great Hall Sunday morning program open to tenth-, eleventh-, and twelfth-graders who wish to continue a kind of post-ninth-grade Sunday morning grouping. As such, it parallels adult worship. Youth attend either the "confirmation/commissioning" or "postcommissioning" classes while adults worship. Jack, the youth minister, says "postcommissioning" is an "awkward name, at best a designation, just barely a description of what happens. We need a name that doesn't have 'post' in it; 'post' has a negative connotation" (tape 12, p.14). An adult speaks to the reasons behind such a class:

> It came about because we felt there was a need in our congregation. I don't know what the percentage was, but well over half of our younger commissioned members, once commissioned, aren't active in the church. They don't seem to find a spot. So we were trying to create a spot that would be meaningful for them. We announced this class, and 16 to 20 signed up right away, and most of them have stayed with the class. The age group is basically sophomore in high school. We have some juniors, too, but basically they're tenth-graders. . . . It's evolving as we go along. We set down some guidelines as to what we hoped

> we could provide, but we [a peer ministry staff] didn't have
> a concrete program going into this, and we met every
> Sunday night, and we put together the next week's pro-
> gram, and we try to tap in to what's current and what's
> interesting, and what we think holds their attention. About
> a month ago there had been a suicide at one of the local
> high schools, and so the following Sunday we were getting
> into listening skills, and we sort of based our lesson around
> this suicide, and the listening skills were tied in to this, and
> how you could be a caring listener and more alert. [tape 12,
> pp. 12-13]

The Great Hall is the same multipurpose cement block
walled gymnasium that served the junior highs as Teen
Center on Friday night. On Sunday morning the same
basketball backboards hang from every wall, and a large
scoreboard dominates one end of the gym. Portable six-
foot dividers split this space into two "confirmation/com-
missioning" and "postcommissioning" classes. No attempts
are made to personalize the space. Cement block walls
dominate the setting.

While attendance at these classes likely replaces worship,
the ninth- and tenth-grade adolescents come dressed exactly the same as most of the adults who attend worship.
Wearing suits, ties, skirts, and "dresses that were almost
party dresses" (tape 21A, p. 14), everyone is well groomed,
including two young men wearing wool sweaters, slacks,
and expensive leather-topped running shoes. The only
blue jeans in sight (worn by one young man) obviously have
been a recent purchase.

Over a twenty minute span on any given Sunday morning, people enter the Great Hall and mill around in small
clusters of conversation. Playing with a "yo-ball," a round
version of a "yo-yo," one young woman interacts with two
young men while another youth purchases a doughnut
from a junior high salesman. Sitting in chairs, three youth
quietly await the start of class. No one touches anyone else.
While the format, space, and personnel for both classes
seem similar, the confirmation/commissioning class has

thirty-five youth in attendance, and the postcommissioning class has twenty. One staff member says: "We have fifty-four ninth graders total if they all come at once, but usually about thirty or forty people come; it's a big class" (tape 7, p. 12).

A total of eight youth and adults carrying materials can be identified readily as those having the leadership responsibilities for the confirmation/commissioning class. When enough youth are present, this staff has a final huddle until a woman in her mid-thirties calls out, "OK, let's get going." Over the next ten minutes, latecomers drift into both groups.

Using the chalkboard, an adult male staffer presents an overview of what has been covered in the class in recent weeks. This is followed by a high school male senior's (the pastor's son) presentation of new material. Splitting into five small groups, each led by one or two staffers, the youth discuss the presentations (historical time-lines related to the Reformation) with seeming animation, each table group engaging in lively conversation. At least two of the tables discuss what happened at McDonald's the previous evening. During this process, an "Attendance Lady" enters, counts heads, collects money placed in an offering plate, and leaves. After twenty minutes of discussion, the class members stand in a circle, announcements are made, a prayer is said by one of the adults, and the class ends. One youth staffer states: "You need to know we don't usually have only a stand-up lecture. We usually get the small groups involved in skits or something like the symbols we made last week, using cardboard kinds of stuff" (tape 21A, p. 13).

After class, conversations continue. One such conversation centers on a youth staffer who had been dropped from the staff because he had quit coming. Some follow-up attention had been planned, but when his sister, present this morning, is asked how he is, the sister's response is, "Wrong question!" So the issue is dropped, at least for the moment. Several staff members set a meeting date during the coming week in order to check class plans for the next several Sundays. Persons in attendance gradually trail off, some with parents who are leaving the worship service, others riding home with older youth.

Peer Ministry Staff

The confirmation/commissioning and post/commissioning classes current leadership model involves young people in active "peer ministry" with other youth. Composed of both youth and adults, two of whom are elders, this "peer ministry staff" is the "latest step in the evolution of St. Andrew's youth ministry leadership process" (tape 8, p. 1). Twenty-five years ago one minister (the only minister) at St. Andrew's taught the confirmation/commissioning class. In 1977 a second man was called to serve and was charged with the responsibility to teach this class. Unable to locate a reasonable class time, this second staff person finally said, "Let's do it on Sunday morning, and let's do it with lay people." He continues: "So we did, and I thought it worked really well. I was in with them maybe once a month for the entire hour. Portions of other times I'd help with the worship service first, and then go to class" (tape 8, p. 2).

With the arrival of Jack, the current youth minister/ choir director and third pastor, the "peer ministry staff" of lay people (including youth and elders) was initiated. The 1983 *Annual Church Report* summarized the peer ministry concept in this way:

> The peer staff meets on a weekly basis to plan lessons, to decide who will be the primary person each Sunday, to share feelings and concerns about the class, and to grow together in faith, as peer ministers. Each Sunday, peer staff members take responsibility to lead and instruct small groups of commissioning class students. The real beauty of this model is that it involves youth teaching, listening, and leading other youth. [p. 17]

Jack invested much time and effort in this initial year of the peer ministry staff with the confirmation/commissioning class. A key training move was a staff retreat. Anne, a youth staffer, remembers:

> We just had a ball. I knew some of the people just slightly and I didn't know one of them at all. And there we were just getting to know one another, and on the retreat after dinner, we sat down on the couch and we talked until 2 A.M., and Jack was there sitting on the floor, and he said, "When are you kids going to sleep?" But we were just having so much fun getting to know each other. So I think we're really compatible, and we worked well together, and you know, we were concerned about each other, too. So I think if the peer ministry staff has a positive feeling for each other they can pass it on to the kids in the class. [tape 5, pp. 2-3]

On that retreat, curriculum ideas were explored and assigned to specific "teams," in order to initiate possibilities for Sunday morning sessions. As the Sunday class got started, "the peer ministry staff carried many responsibilities, but none greater," said Anne, "than what happened when one of the peer staff members was absent. I'd call and say, 'How've you been? We need you. Is there something I can help you with? Can you share with me the reason you can't come?' You know, things like that are important" (tape 5, p. 3).

When asked to symbolically draw an image of youth ministry at St. Andrew's, Anne drew "a bunch of people all gathered around a table, sharing together. In my drawing, the bread and the wine are important. Because I think every time we sat down together, as a staff, we had a sort of communion with each other" (tape 6, p. 4). For Anne this sense of communion "spilled over into the people in the class, too. They felt it because we were all so concerned about each other" (tape 5, p. 4).

Anne noted that being on peer ministry staff had some negative moments, too. These usually were tied to her expectations over how important a particular day's lesson should be:

> There was a time when, boy, did I get mad because nobody
> seemed to care . . . It was one of those days when the lesson
> was really important, or at least I thought it was . . . and they
> didn't . . . and I just had to sit back and go, "well, you guys,
> if you really want to talk and not listen, go ahead; but I really
> worked hard on this, and I'm getting angry because you
> don't want to listen to me at all." [tape 5, p. 4]

Anne expected some of this to happen; but when it did,
it still was tough! Overall Anne felt that things worked
better with a peer staff because members "had a lot in
common and there was a lot to talk about. And we'd usually
get into our lesson because they would come up and say to
me, 'What are we doing today?' And I would say in fun,
'You have to wait and see.' Cause there's usually something
fun to do, you know" (tape 5, p. 5).

Anne, one of the initial peer staff members and by all
accounts a good one, also was involved in the youth choir,
regular Sunday worship, the hand-bell choir, the occasional
church orchestra, and deacons. Eventually Anne dropped
out of the peer ministry staff, even though she enjoyed it,
because she "had school activities, too" (tape 5, p. 3). "My
mom says, 'You have to!' So . . . I did" (tape 5, p. 4). The
dilemma Anne faced is noted by one elder who served as a
youth peer staffer. She comments that the program is
excellent and she wants it to continue, but

> I saw strain on some of our peer staff. We had one excellent
> peer staff member [Anne], and she quit this year because
> she's a senior, and she knew she could not handle it and
> struggle to get through her senior year. And I totally
> understand that, and I guess I work hard for it not to be a
> strain for our peer staff. For them it's real; they feel the
> strain. [tape 2, pp. 25-26]

This "strain" is very much on the minds of those adult
advisors who work (without a peer staff) with the Sunday
evening fellowship group.

One advisor shares his bottom line:

Some of the kids amaze me with their candor. They wouldn't talk to anybody else except Jack and myself about these things. I'd like to think it's because we've made this a place where they know it's gonna stay confidential. It's safe here, if they're having trouble with their folks or if they are having trouble at school, they can talk to us. We aren't gonna lecture them, we aren't gonna turn them over to the cops or whatever. [tape 3, p. 8]

Youth initially come to Senior High Fellowship "because everyone comes" (tape 3, p. 5); but here, among these fifteen to twenty youth, grade and school cliques from Crest and Jameson appear to break down as the year progresses. By midyear a youth can sum it up in these words: "It's like a big circle with a lot of little circles inside of it. The big circle would be the fellowship and the little circle would be the little groups we're trying to get together" (tape 3, p. 6).

There is no evidence of a shared overt religious language or the articulated need for one within any of these groups (commissioning, postcommissioning, peer staff, youth fellowship). The problem is, one advisor confesses, "We tend to leave the spiritual things more or less to Jack, and he's the one that does the 'let's have a symbol of this,' because we're not very good at that" (tape 12, p. 4). She also suggests: "I don't think these kids are very spiritual. I know that's just my opinion, but we've decided that if we get too heavy at all about those kinds of things, then we'd lose them. So we have Jack kind of sneak some of that stuff in a little bit" (tape 12, pp. 6-7). In part this is a reaction to the literal "God-talk" language of the many "conservative" churches located in the area (tape 15A, pp. 6-7); but it is also an honest reflection of the youth advisors' understanding of religion as a horizontal human fellowship. This is best summed up with one advisor's comment: "I think just by our coming here and getting together and chatting and having a good time we celebrate. If we go out on something, nobody's ever been bored on anything we've gone on—ever. And we're going on a hayride tomorrow night. It'll be a wild time" (tape 3, p. 9). Apparently those youth in attendance agree with this "horizontal" assessment. In commenting on worship, one states, "I think just being together is enough celebration" (tape 5, p. 11).

Jack and the Senior High Fellowship advisors are committed to doing "service projects" with the youth. One advisor puts it like this:

> We're at the point now where we're starting to do some service projects. We're going to try and raise some money to buy some kind of heating devices for the Northside Team Ministry and they are scraping along on a shoestring so we get the youth involved in that sort of thing. We're also going to try and sponsor a couple of families this year at Christmas time. The youth will set up a Christmas tree out in the hallway with tags on it describing clothes or whatever. People fill the tree and boxes with clothes and then we're gonna take them down to deliver. I think what is really important about that is that we get these guys involved personally. We took the youth on a Walk for Hunger last spring and we walked past some of the housing projects and some of the youth were gonna be cocky and make jokes about it, just a psychological type of response, but a lot of them just sort of quietly walked by. Frankly, I think they were scared. They just didn't realize what goes on out there. If nothing else Jack and I would really like to get them to open their eyes, just a little, and realize that something exists besides Crest High School. [tape 3, p. 3]

One senior high youth believes projects like the space heaters, the Hunger Hike, the Heifer Arkansas Project, and the Trip to Chicago are important "eye-openers." She says: "It's sad to say, but that's what they are. All people do not live like we live in Crestwood, you know. And I think such trips and projects give people a chance to start being aware of that and start helping to make a dent in the problem" (tape 5, p. 7).

CHAPTER
THREE

DOUBLE VISION: PROGRAM DIRECTOR OR RITUAL ELDER?

Interviewer: So what's ministry at St. Andrew's all about anyway?

Jack [youth minister]: I don't know. I think this church kind of lost its vision. Ministry here is how well you administer church programs. It [the church] really has very little to say.

Interviewer: Say more about ministry.

Jack: Ministry here nurtures without any sharp edges. If you make "religious" noises, you don't fit. And everyone here fits. I mean, these are nice people here, but they want programs to be better informed, or to learn a new skill. They don't want to change things.

tape 15A, p. 25.

In the mid-1970s a past chairperson of the Christian education board remembers many members of St. Andrew's saying "we need something for the youth of this church" (tape 2, p. 19). At that time the church had 450 to 500 members. A second professional minister had been hired for Christian education, but church members were expressing their need to have someone on board to be responsible for youth. At that time the Junior High and Senior High Fellowship groups were struggling. Volunteers could not provide continuity. Resources—people with creative ideas—were absent. While this was at a point when the church was rapidly expanding, youth were barely tolerated:

"They were here and that's it, you know. It was disappointing" (tape 1, p. 5).

The youth committee was a subcommittee of the Christian education board and did not meet with regularity. One person remembers that even though an elder of the church headed the youth committee, he "only had one meeting in an entire year because he said [laughter] there was nothing to do. Nothing to do" (tape 1, p. 7). At the same time the youth choir was struggling. The entire youth program of St. Andrew's was "in poor health" (tape 1, p. 7).

In the 1978 *Congregational Long-Range Planning Report*, two of the adopted top three goals were youth-oriented. An elder of the church at that time remembers thinking "that big a priority ought to have its own board" (tape 8, p. 3). And there was a group of laypersons who chose to express their concern by supporting such a move. With this support "and with the church continuing to expand, the board of Christian education elevated the youth committee to board status. This seems a logical solution to the expanding responsibilities of both groups" (tape 2, p. 20). This was a way of declaring priorities; if you will, a symbolic declaration: "By so doing we were saying youth ministry is important to us—so important that we are going to have a board" (tape 9, p. 7). An active search ensued for a youth minister. The *Church Profile* distributed at that time summed up the congregation's concern about youth in this fashion:

> This congregation has been and will continue to be actively concerned about involving young people in the believing community. Society pulls and tugs and in flashy ways tries to attract youth to secular and sometimes destructive pursuits. We want the gospel to speak to them in meaningful ways, so that their commitment is to Christ and his way. [*Church Profile*, 1981]

In attempting to define the St. Andrew's concept of youth minister, the 1981 youth minister profile prioritized "pastoral activities" for the youth minister in the following manner (number 1, highest priority):

1. Spiritual development of members
2. Counseling services
3. Development and support of educational program
4. Teaching responsibility
5. Administrative leadership

Using the same categories, we asked and received the senior pastor's ranking (1985):

1. Development and support of educational program
2. Teaching responsibility
3. Counseling services
4. Administrative leadership
5. Spiritual development of members

In addition, we received the youth minister's ranking (1985):

1. Administrative leadership
2. Development and support of education program
3. Teaching responsibility
4. Counseling services
5. Spiritual development of members

While laity specifically ranked "spiritual development of members" as their number one priority, neither the senior pastor nor the youth minister did so; both placed the spiritual development of members as their final priority. While the senior minister said "administrative leadership" *should be* the top priority, the youth minister's rationale for his ranking was that a primary role for him (spiritual development) was not actually expected of him. There is, in both ministers' rankings, a subtle recognition of two different visions. The clash of these two visions ultimately led Jack, the youth minister, to resign his youth ministry position at St. Andrew's.

Jack's Dilemma

What follows is an edited interview with Jack, subsequently read and approved by him:

> **Jack:** When you talk about ultimates here in Crestwood, ultimates are the education. Ultimates are success socially. But real ultimates for me include realizing that you're a finite creature; that you don't decide your birth and your death; that you live dependent; you are not independent. Who is it, I can't remember, Dominick Crossan, I think, who said that "really reading and understanding the gospel is like going down a white water river on a raft with no life preserver."

> **Interviewer:** Yeah, but here are folk who have come out of hard scrabble times and have made it to Crestwood via education. . . .

> **Jack:** Right, that was what got them out of the wilderness.

> **Interviewer:** So what happens at St. Andrew's?

> **Jack:** Let me answer that this way. Two years ago one of the first retreats occurred where I started really looking at discipleship. I did a process where we experienced what binds us in our lives with ropes, literally trying us in knots, with me ultimately cutting off each rope with a knife "in the name of Jesus Christ."

> **Interviewer:** The way you say that sounds like you scared 'em to death.

> **Jack:** That's true. And I heard so much flack from the parents who said "What did you do out there?" You know, "What did you do to those kids," "Wow, that was heavy," "How can you do that?"

> **Interviewer:** You mean, like "How can you do this to my kid?"

> **Jack:** Yes, and they're saying, "if this is Christianity, I don't want to be a part of it." I know it's a risk to have kids sit there and have them think, while bound together, about symbols

of the binding grasp of society on your lives, the culture, the peers, you know, what the cultural life does to us. And yet, as a creature of God we can experience God's love and can be freed from those bonds . . . no matter what culture binds us.

Interviewer: No matter what culture . . . you are saying that you don't have to be bound; and by cutting the rope with the knife and saying, "Know that the grace of God. . . ."

Jack: ". . . has made you free." You are transformed, a new being!

Interviewer: It seems to me that in that moment *you* really experienced something of what the prophetic and the priestly aspects of ministry are all about in a very, *for you*, powerful and meaningful way.

Jack: And that was enjoyable to me . . . I loved it. It was one of the most memorable experiences I've had. But because of the negative reaction that I received from the majority of the adults, I saw it as a rejection of my being a "priest" in ministry. As I think about it now, it *was* rejection, it was saying we want our kids to get together for fun times, the enjoyable times, but we don't want them to have a lot of religious depth. We want to be surface and shallow, and don't bring that religious stuff in; leave it out on the doorstep.

Interviewer: Jack, in another related area, we find in the tapes symbols again and again of safety. We also noted that's what Crestwood's Principal was talking about today—that parents want the school to provide safety. So that when kids go to school they're going to get in a safe track, and at the end they're going to safely get to Yale and everyone knows what's going to happen *exactly*.

Jack: Well, I can understand where they're coming from, but that isn't the way people grow or live, and that certainly isn't going down a rapids in a raft without a life preserver.

Interviewer: Maybe what we see could be called the clash of the priestly or prophetic role of the church with what you perceive as a too easy acceptance of the culture?

Jack: Yes, and it's frustrating. It's very frustrating. To have to work in that clash is frustrating.

Interviewer: Let me push you further on this. In your own understanding of where you stand as a minister, does that include picking up on the religious language and the priestly mantle and doing more priestly kinds of things? Is that something that you now want to *own* as a part of your ministry?

Jack: Well, it's important but it's not feasible.

Interviewer: It's not feasible for you personally?

Jack: It's not feasible for me in this particular setting. I mean, that's part of my calling. But there's no sense claiming it here. There's no feeling for it by me here. [tape 15A, pp. 18-24]

When first hired, Jack had responded to the youth minister profile (1981) that specifically noted that the person called as youth minister should consider him/herself as a pastor *first*. In addition, the youth minister was "to understand [that] the senior pastor is the head of staff and that the Associate may be asked to carry out other duties at the direction of the senior pastor" (*Youth Minister Profile*, 1981). The senior pastor was quite clear on this final point: "We'll talk, we'll share, we'll reflect and try to come to a mutual understanding on any issue, but if we come to a crunch point, I've got 51 percent of the vote, and you know, I know, I'm not an overbearing person" (tape 20, p. 17). While not leading any ongoing programs himself, the senior pastor provides through his staff of associates as many program opportunities as possible, to as many people as possible, in order that they might become more familiar with the church, and ultimately, more committed to it.

Each program is seen by the senior pastor as a potential entryway into stronger membership. For example, if a nonmember adult agrees to chaperon at Teen Center one Friday evening, certain questions might come alive that might lead that chaperon to an adult class or to conversations with the pastor, and perhaps ultimately to membership. Consequently, the senior pastor relies upon what he calls a "cafeteria" model of the church "in terms of ministry" (tape 20, p. 11). By "cafeteria" is meant that a variety of possibilities are offered along the church's menu line. People can pick and choose—that is, "one could load up in desserts and skip the meat and potatoes" (tape 20, p. 11). But that is a risk the senior pastor is willing to take. He states:

> You know, I don't find the cafeteria model all that bad. There may be some models that are better, but at least one of the things that has occurred over the . . . let's see, I've been here fifteen years now . . . is we've been able to constantly build on the program and offer more possibilities. And parents respond. If they feel like the church is providing something for their kids, well then "whew!" . . . And they relax, because there's a couple of items on the menu that their kids can eat, and I've covered my responsibility by knowing that it's there and they can respond and are going to respond. [tape 20, p. 12]

Not personally leading any of the ongoing programs, the senior pastor coordinates the male associate pastors who supervise existing and emerging programs. An associate pastor indicates such programs are the primary way an associate pastor's time gets spent:

> Every time you start a new program, that's more staff time. I don't care how many people are running the program, very confident lay people, it's still staff time. It's gotta be. There's no way it runs on its own steam; somebody's got to oversee that program. There's time commitment whether it's related to building, whether it be related to scheduling, whether it be related to programing, resourcing, whether it be related to conflicts that are produced within it. No, you name it, anything that is sponsored by this church, somebody on the professional staff has to be related to it. [tape 16, p. 17]

In addition to assuming the youth minister's position, Jack also assumed the role of youth choir director. An adult notes: "I was on the committee when we had to hire a choir director and at the same time we were looking for a youth minister, and Jack wanted to combine music with his ministry, and we all wondered whether it would work. But the unique part of it is that his ministry of music has fed into the youth ministry" (tape 10, pp. 11-12).

Stress and the Youth Minister

Having the dual role of youth minister and youth choir director, Jack works with four choirs: "Proclamation, a youth vocal choir for grades 7-12; Joyful Ringers, a hand-bell choir for grades 7-8; Celebration Ringers, a hand-bell choir for grades 9-12; and Proclamation Ringers, a select hand-bell choir for grades 9-12" (*St. Andrew's Youth Ministry Bulletin*). This is in addition to the youth minister's job description:

> The person will be directly responsible for Youth Ministry, which includes the Senior High Youth Fellowship (a high priority), the Junior High Youth Fellowship (a high priority), the Commissioning Class (a high priority), Teen Center, Scouts, God and Country Program, Recreation/Athletics, and other youth programs that may be developed. The youth minister will work with the Christian education committee and the youth committee. New programs are anticipated with young adults, both singles and college students. This person will preach twelve times each year, engage in calling as coordinated by the head pastor, serve as a liturgist, perform weddings and funerals, and share responsibility for general communication. As an associate, this minister will work closely with the other two pastors.
> [*Youth Minister Profile*, 1987]

Each choir meets during the week for practice and performs regularly in Sunday worship.

Aware of many youth stresses, Jack consciously viewed each choir practice as a minifellowship group. Tending to be relaxed and accepting of much giggling and interaction, Jack's approach to rehearsals appeared to bring in more youth. One church member commented:

> Before Jack came, our youth choir, Junior High and Senior High combined, ran 12 to 15 people. We now have, I would say, 35 or 40. Last year we ran out of robes and we frantically tried to put together robes. We're out of robes again, so this year they're just singing in their Sunday clothes because we have to pick up some more robes again . . . somewhere!! [tape 10, p. 7]

The visibility of these youth choirs in worship has, in the eyes of many parishioners, validated Jack as youth minister. One parishioner explains:

> I really think that our young people have been doing a lot more things since Jack's been here. Sometimes you think maybe it's because you weren't so involved, but I see . . . just sitting back in church, there's more choirs, the hand bells, you just see kids doing so much more in the church, and I think it's because he spends the time. My daughter who is 16, well, you would think that she would be getting away from the church, but she's probably doing more now than she did before. [tape 12, p. 2]

Jack explains that it was not easy sorting out the relationship between his roles of choir director and youth minister. Such a dual role can be complex. Jack started out as a fairly authoritative choir director and as an open and accessible youth minister. After a particularly rough series of choir practices, some folk in the Senior High Fellowship used that group's overnight "lock-in" to vent feelings about Jack's role as choir director/youth minister. One youth choir member emerged from that discussion convinced that Jack was "trapped by the dual roles" (tape 8, p. 3); but Jack emerged with a different viewpoint:

> I found that my concern for the kids, my ministry, spilled over into choir. I sacrificed some discipline and made the

rehearsals more laid back, more friendly, more of a community kind of thing. In a way, each choir is a small youth group. Sometimes we get really into the music and really work; at other times we get giddy and take a break and play games in the Great Hall. And I'm not so worried about the discipline of the choir. I'm worried about the cultural stresses on the kids. And so far, it's worked. We do okay. [tape 27, p. 10]

A youth choir member's perceptions of this is that choir members are "still not disciplined enough, but I think that's one of the problems we've been addressing in choir. Jack wanted us to really dig in and everybody else wants to talk a little bit, you know. But Jack's eased off, and we're working harder, so I think we're starting to reach a happy medium" (tape 5, p. 12).

After Jack's involvement over three years, the youth program was highly visible. One parent expressed it this way, "Our goals are being met. I have to give Jack an awful lot of credit. Everything that St. Andrew's kept asking for—it's finally here" (tape 2, pp. 18-19).

Nevertheless, while many laypersons were pleased with the programs offered, others, knowing the size and comprehensiveness of the youth minister's job description, plus the added area of the youth choirs and the continued emphasis on program expansion, wondered about the load Jack carried:

I don't know how he juggles it, because he does the commissioning class, the postcommissioning class, the senior high fellowship, the junior high fellowship, is involved with the young adults class, does bell choirs and vocal groups for service, and supervises them all and keeps them working. To talk to some of the older kids in the senior high fellowship before Jack got here, there was almost nothing and in, how long's he been here, 2 1/2 years maybe, yeah, he came here shortly before we moved to town, and in that time he's going from almost nothing to a very vital youth program. It's always something going on. He even has his thumb in the basketball program, doing something with that. I don't know how he keeps it all straight. He doesn't know how he keeps it all straight sometimes. [tape 3, pp. 11-12]

Jack agreed with this assessment, particularly because "what's important at St. Andrew's is to develop the program, and what happens is that I end up developing and maintaining it for them" (tape 19, p. 14). At midpoint in our year of observations, a senior high youth described Jack's potential burnout:

> Jack is overextended. Jack is in charge of the youth program, and he can't do all this stuff all at once, so a lot of the stuff doesn't get done if he doesn't do it. And he can't handle it all. And the people we have teaching, they are overextended, too. Cause, you know, they have so many other commitments. And Jack's a nice guy, but sometimes when all this stuff falls down on him and he gets sort of on the warpath, then he just doesn't have time for anything. And he's just involved with everything, and he doesn't have time, you know? Plus he's got his family . . . and he needs more help. I think Jack's getting burned out, and when that happens there'll be all these people running around like chickens with their heads cut off. [tape 7, pp. 20-21]

In all of this, Jack's professional associate noted: "We're gonna be burned out, we're gonna suffer stress . . . we've got to reward ourselves once in a while. And that's part of the leadership that comes down to us. I don't think the three of us on staff are really super about giving each other strokes. I think all three of us can do better . . . to one another and also to laypeople" (tape 8, p. 6).

Jack resigned at the close of our year of research, and as he prepared to leave St. Andrew's, the senior pastor initiated a new staff member search. At one point in the search he attempted to steer the description of the open position toward that of youth "director"—that is, finding someone who did not have ministerial training to "manage" the youth program at St. Andrew's. The laity rejected this move, remaining firmly committed to hiring an ordained minister (Interviewer's Journal, June 1985).

CHAPTER
FOUR

EMBRACING DOMINANT CULTURE

In the last hundred years or so, particularly in connection with the development of a modern industrial and post-industrial economy, the emphasis has increasingly been on a kind of purely individual achievement—upward mobility, leaving home, leaving the community where you grew up, the church you were raised in, going to school, competing for good grades, going somewhere else to take a job, getting transferred over here, going on ideally to greater and greater stardom—more money, more titles, etc.

That is very lonesome. Not only don't you need other people, in the same way you are constantly competing with other people.

Robert N. Bellah[1]

While human beings are always interpreting their world, a case can be made that adolescents are particularly involved in trying to make sense out of their experience. There are developmental reasons for this: by eleven or twelve a child who once assumed that everyone saw the world in the same way now has the ability to think abstractly. With this newfound ability comes the recognition that people see things differently. About the same time, a child who once operated as if time existed only within the present "now," begins to wrestle with the idea of a personal future.

In similar fashion, a child who once could only understand the world as containing a certain neighborhood or town, begins to expand the idea of space to include other countries and galaxies. As such developmental changes occur, other interpretive possibilities open up for the growing adolescent.

The Interpretive Process of Adolescence

It is also during adolescence when youth begin to commit themselves, in ways that shape their personal identities, to certain ideas, institutions, and persons.[2] This makes adolescence an appropriate time for the church to proclaim to and with youth, in as full-orbed a way as possible, its kerygmatic claim that "Jesus is the Christ." *Kerygma* is ministry articulated; it is the proclamation of the good news of salvation in all possible ways. There are many "kerygmas," however, and kerygmatic claims are often grounded in sources other than Jesus Christ.

Other claims are often seductive, if not compelling. For example, viewing a thirty-second video telling an adolescent to "be all that you can be," immerses the viewer in the powerful symbol system of the military community. The viewer sees good-looking men and women wearing attractive uniforms, hears martial, upbeat, exciting music, and tastes the possibility of being tested in war. For thirty seconds the adolescent interpretively pursues the question, "Is 'being a soldier' something to which I can be faithful?"

When pressed, every community has similar sets of relatively *objective* communal symbols, implicitly and explicitly stewarded by the ritual elders of those communities.[3] Such symbols expand and contract as the community interacts in an ongoing *subjective* interpretive process. There are many such communities of interpretation within our culture; the church is only one such community.

Steven Jones, in *Faith Shaping: Youth and the Experience of Faith*, offers us a story regarding the clash of two such interpretive communities. Jones met a woman who assured him that it was her intention not to influence her children regarding faith, which she assumed was an *adult* issue. As

Jones visited her home, he quickly surmised that she "prized an academic, scientific worldview that, in fact, matched her own faith commitments, and her children were deeply steeped in that faith bias."[4] As Jones is quick to point out, we indeed *immerse* our children in those perspectives, worldviews, values, and commitments we ourselves honor. And we tend to gravitate into communities of kindred souls.

As diverse communities generate their own interpretive ways of looking at and being in the world, differing patterns, feelings, loyalties, and ways of being come to be honored by particular adolescents. Craig Dykstra has noted that we do not have to concoct special programs to entice adolescents into this ongoing interpretive process. Children, youth, and adolescents are all naturally immersed in such a process. What we have to do, Dykstra contends, is "to develop a religious pattern of interpretation that is both biblical and illuminating of contemporary human experience. Furthermore, our task is to help young people experiment with this pattern of interpretation, understand it, and increasingly adopt it as their own in the context of a community of interpretation that does the same with them."[5]

Social entities encompassing time and space, churches are natural, historical, human enterprises, full-blown communities of interpretation.[6] The church's communal signs and systems seem to be relatively available and, in addition, relatively concrete, consisting of, for example, hymns, chalices, liturgies, confessions, biblical metaphors and themes, art and architectural forms, historical events, and persons of faith. These, and other objective "marks" of the community, however, are either *implicitly* or *explicitly* interpreted to its members, particularly to those just moving into membership.

Noting that it is only through an intentional interpretive process that the past becomes a living part of a community's present, James M. Gustafson underscores the need for an *explicit* community process of interpretation: "[Interpreters] must understand the meaning of the sign and [they] must understand the persons to whom [they are] interpreting if [they are] to be effective. The church is a community of interpretation. The signs interpreted mark the differentiation between it and other communities."[7] *Objective* in form, such "signs" have a "life," an evocative existence of their own. When and wherever Christians gather, these are the universals that appear. They constitute the particularity of a given church, however, only insofar as they express the *subjective* "collective consciousness" of that community.[8] When such symbols are powerfully embodied within a local context, adolescent lifestyles and identities are impacted, personal commitments are made, transformations occur, and communal experience is altered.

Using these understandings of how a community interprets its existence, I am struck by St. Andrew's uneasiness about making any interpretations in conjunction with the "objective" symbols of the Christian faith. Not only do the laypeople admit their inability to refer, in any transformative or useful way, to the words, themes, and symbols of the Christian faith, they also appear to have unreflectively accepted certain signs and symbols from the broader "American" culture as the commonly agreed upon "marks" of their faith community. The symbols of the dominant culture therefore seem to provide the interpretive framework for this church. It is also clear, to a considerable extent, that the professional staff of St. Andrew's have reached a similar resolution regarding the role of the church in that culture, and vice versa.

It is my contention that a faithful youth ministry enters the interpretive process of adolescence at the point of the tension that *always* exists between the Christian gospel and the culture in which we are immersed. When there is *no* tension, then youth "ministry" becomes little more than a cultural manual, a handbook of strategies for cultural success. In this respect, I agree with Michael Warren, who argues that we often, in the name of the gospel, "hand on to young people the vision of the dominant culture, covered over with a thin religious veneer."[9]

Unfortunately, the stress of being white, middle-class, and adolescent within a church accepting this culture's interpretive symbology is painfully evident at St. Andrew's. For example, while the American myth suggests that everyone in our society starts on equal footing, the youth of St. Andrew's come to understand, through a kind of implicit or "hidden" cultural curriculum, that social order is arrived at and maintained through intense *competition.*

It is here, perhaps, that one looks for a contrary theme to be provided from the Reformed tradition of this church. But it is as if St. Andrew's has given up that role; almost as if it has seen its Reformed tradition accepted, embraced by the dominant culture and retranslated in barbaric form. Martin Marty suggests that "the American way of life . . . creates a kind of envelope of meanings which rejects or overwhelms signals (of Reformed America) setting out to produce an America Reformed."[10] Thus, individuals "succeed" in life by "winning": they competitively climb the ladders in high school, attend the right colleges, and receive the professional corporation positions that will reward their continued competition. To achieve the status, comfort, and individual security associated with such an American middle-class existence is the expected reward for the St. Andrew's adolescents successfully persevering in this competitive spirit. But this process depends upon *competition* as its foremost value—even after successfully "arriving," the middle-class adults of St. Andrew's must maintain a high level of competitive "worth"—or suffer the consequences.

At St. Andrew's, such powerful cultural understandings permeate the climate adolescents breathe daily. In school ("Crest is best"), the formal vehicle socializing and enculturating St. Andrew's adolescents, the dilemma of honoring mutually contradictory values of "equality" and "individual achievement" is resolved with the stressing of "competition" and "fair play." The resulting "class rank" (a central factor for college acceptance) is then understood to be the normal outcome of working hard in school, and by inference, working toward "success" in our society.

The Crestwood High School principal, Dr. Cardinal, was unusually candid in his remarks about Crest. He felt Crest was "a stressful place with a lot of selections. If you settle in and work hard, you'll do well. If you can't settle in, you drop, and drop hard" (tape 17, p. 26). "Crest is best," the motto of those attending Crestwood High School (and St. Andrew's Church), summarizes the competitive, individualistic, hierarchical code of the white, middle class:

> The cultural system of class thus depends upon the secular nature of the social order, on the predominance of the person rather than the group as the unit which is conceptualized and evaluated in the system, on the value of equality predominating over (though not eliminating) the value of hierarchy, and upon the premise that the person is, or should be, autonomous. That is, he [sic] should be free to pursue his [sic] ends in a rational manner, unencumbered by family, fate or station in life.[11]

Thus, the adolescents of St. Andrew's receive the "signs and symbols" of their "community of faith" (a white, American middle-class ethos) primarily through mandatory attendance at the local high school. Here is where they will be socialized into the important values and patterns of living that will effectively guide them into middle-class existence.

How the Dominant Culture "Captures" Youth

Crestwood High School provides something for everybody. As a modern, up-to-date, high school, "Crest" offers great variety, but rarely presses students to choose wisely or engage deeply. This occurs, in large part, because the *experience* of being in school is more important than any depthful pursuit of education. There is, some critics suggest, a deliberate approach on the part of public high schools to accommodate great diversity in topical offerings, "so that students will stay on, graduate, and be happy."[12] Such accommodation within the mandatory framework of the school provides an "educative" environment where adolescents get to do their own thing: here "pluralism," and the attendant virtues of tolerance and diversity, have come to preclude the notion of "schools' celebrating more focused notions of education or of character. 'Community' has come to mean differences peacefully coexisting rather than people working together toward some serious end."[13] Such accommodations, say some, betray the public high schools' real connection to the economic/socialization needs of this culture, and make many of the "better" high schools strongly resemble shopping malls.[14]

We forget, or fail to understand, that "Crest" is the end result of a variety of factors that coalesced over time into the public high school—that is, what we today consider as the normal place where adolescents "spend" most of their time. If Crestwood High School provides most of the interpretive symbols and signs for today's adolescents, how such occurred and what some of these "signs" are should be of great importance to those who work with America's youth. To "unpack" the contemporary high school, we must journey back in time.

There was no mandatory public high school system in the early 1800s in America. This did not mean that students were not involved in the educational process. For example, those in the state of Massachusetts could attend a wide variety of free or tuition-charging private schools, academies, town schools, and other institutions providing specialized educational services. The Sunday school was one such "free" school. In 1817 the Boston Society petitioned for the Sunday use of a grammar school in an area bordering Boston Commons that contained many lower-class, foreign-born, and black families.[15] The society intended, through the Sunday school format, "to reclaim the vicious, to instruct the ignorant, to secure the observance of the Sabbath, to induce the children to attend public worship, and to raise the standard of morals among the lower classes of society."[16] By 1837, when the Massachusetts legislature set up a board of education, the Boston Sabbath School Union enrolled 12,602 regular students with 376 volunteer teachers.[17]

Despite the fact that institutions like the Sunday school were firmly in place and doing a credible job, this eclectic mix of educational vehicles was judged by Horace Mann to be inadequate for the task of socializing youth into modern American society. Secretary from 1837 to 1847 of the newly formed Massachusetts Board of Education, Mann saw the more orthodox wing of the church and the sudden influx of Roman Catholic immigrants as factors representing values and traditions detrimental to a more positive and liberal formation of citizens. Mann's antidote was to affirm a state-mandated and -supported "common school" anchored in a common core of white, Protestant, middle-class, liberal values. This school was to be attended by *all* children within an identifiable area, and as Charles Leslie Glenn Jr. argues in *The Myth of the Common School*, was to shape rough-hewn citizens into a "common culture," which eliminated "the subcultures of creed, locality, or tradition to which many parents gave their loyalty. . . . They represented the societal 'center' in its attempt to integrate the various peripheries of an expanding society."[18] In the face of "the immigrant threat" and the subsequent Roman Catholic expansion, liberal and conservative Protestants closed ranks in support of Mann's "common school."[19] Someone like Horace Bushnell, author of *Discourses in*

Christian Nurture (Boston: Sabbath School Society, 1847), came to affirm the "common school" for the following reasons: (1) private schools were dangerous; (2) parochial schools were un-American; (3) Americans were a Protestant people; (4) the state has the right and responsibility to control the education of its citizenry; and (5) the common school would create social cohesion.[20]

Joining forces, most Protestant denominations fully supported the common school while abandoning their own private schools, concentrating instead upon the establishment of colleges for the training of teachers.[21] Set up to educate and prepare teachers for the common school, these "normal" colleges interestingly were referred to as "teacher seminaries."[22] Given the fact that the ranks of the Protestants had closed behind what Mann saw as a religious "crusade," this was a fair description. As Glenn depicts the American public's embrace of the common school, "It became the core institution of American society, the definer of meanings, and the only way to higher life—spiritually as well as materially—for generations of immigrant and native-born children alike."[23] The Massachusetts "common school" became a model for the nation. Once fixed in the public mind as the center where social opportunities might be gained, the public "common" school quickly became the major vehicle for social indoctrination as well as social control within this society.

While a variety of forces from the late nineteenth and early twentieth centuries were instrumental in creating the "common" school, none were more powerful than the newly emerging interests of capital, labor, and public welfare. These forces were partially reconciled in the early twentieth century through an ever-expanding economy of production and consumption of goods and services in which public education and the for-profit corporation came to play increasingly key roles. In *Shaping the American Educational State: 1900 to the Present,* Clarence Karier suggests the systemic implications connected to the emerging centrality of education in the United States:

> A part of that system came to include a vast compulsory elementary and secondary educational system, capped by the university. The university played a fundamental role in providing the expertise that created the theoretical and practical knowledge and trained manpower by which the system has been sustained and further developed. In return, the political-economic system invested heavily in a vast educational complex which, from kindergarten to graduate school, served to train producers and consumers, to manage labor supply and, more importantly, to teach those values necessary to maintain the kind of community now in existence.[24]

In the seventy years between 1870 and 1940, the American population trebled, while the American high school population increased ninety times, and the college and university population increased thirty times.[25] "As this educational frontier emerged, a young man would more often be advised to go to college rather than to go West."[26] This new pursuit of education by the emerging middle-class "professional" was disconnected from any religious sense of "calling"; instead, the new, self-made professional embarked on a career: "The goal was no longer the fulfillment of a commonly understood form of life but the attainment of 'success,' and success depended for its very persuasive power on its indefiniteness, its open-endedness, the fact that whatever 'success' one had obtained, one could always obtain more."[27]

Employing the new "professional" was the for-profit corporation, another "invention" that occurred in America following the Civil War. As striving for the American dream became equated with (1) becoming middle-class (a term emergent only in the last decades of the nineteenth century), (2) vertical advancement within a corporation, (3) expanded income, and (4) a utilitarian understanding of education, young men criticized, calculated, and acted with some measure of impunity toward their less flexible elders. "Above all, young men could begin thinking in vertical rather than horizontal imagery. They meant, very literally, to move up and away."[28]

Mainstream denominational churches, for better or for worse, embraced the public high school and the post-Civil War corporation. In an article entitled "The Incorporation of the Presbyterians," Louis B. Weeks indicates how the Presbyterian Church, filled with "typically literate, well-educated, and aspirant" members, rushed to embrace the corporation and its hierarchical, managerial efficiency. Weeks concludes: "Corporations seized the imagination of American culture, moreover, so all our major institutions including churches evolved in the manner of these corporations."[29]

While the liberal Protestant grip on the public schools' "religious mission" began to weaken in the early twentieth century, churches like St. Andrew's continue to invest religious significance in its embrace of middle-class "success" and the role of the high school in socializing youth into the corporate structures of the culture. This framework of interpretation can be said to be anchored by a model of youth ministry that *educates* within a *corporation metaphor.*

Ministry as Education Within a Corporation Metaphor

In a "corporation church," it is "the vertical chain of command that most clearly defines the structure. We understand the top minister as the senior head of staff, the Chief Executive Officer, the CEO who holds the power and gives the orders. He is the 'boss'" (conference tape, p. 2). While large churches need pastors who are effective administrators, "at St. Andrew's the senior pastor seems to be above the task of leading programs; in this process he seems to function less like a pastor and more like a corporation executive. He makes staff decisions and appears in public as the visible person who is 'in charge'; i.e., who regularly preaches and manages the church. He makes it clear that this is a big job" (conference tape, p. 11). Power resides at the top of this corporation's ladder: decisions "are made within a 'top-down' structure in which youth are some of the least powerful persons for whom the church provides educational programs" (conference tape, p.8).

By assuming youth's status as residing in the powerless condition of adolescence, St. Andrew's "maintains a clear understanding of corporate accountability—adults are on top" (conference tape, p. 11). Those who have power at St. Andrew's are adults who have competed and "won" hard fought, middle-class status. Thus, youth ministry at St. Andrew's consists of managing a series of educative programs that occur within an "adult controlled division of the corporation" (conference tape, p. 11). This division, the youth department, is headed by a talented upper-level executive—Jack, a "professional" minister to youth.

Because "transcendent" language is understood at St. Andrew's to equal, in a negative sense, conservative or fundamentalistic religious language, it is the language of management that has become St. Andrew's language of transformation. The use of any transcendent or transformative religious language meets with strong resistance at St. Andrew's. Jack's retreat experience (cutting the bonds that enslaved youth, while calling on the name of Jesus) offered an explicit religious and transcendent image that confronted and reframed youth's cultural existence; as such it was actively resisted by the adults of St. Andrew's. Such transcendent and transformative activity from an admittedly religious perspective was not encouraged at St. Andrew's. Instead, "administrative expertise mixed with managerial savvy is the 'bottom-line secular' language employed throughout the church whenever it meets with the intention of effecting change" (conference tape, p. 7).

The Dilemma Facing Anne

A dilemma associated with this culturally accommodating model of ministry can be illustrated in that the Senior High Fellowship (a regular 15-20 member Sunday evening gathering with Jack and three lay advisors) occasionally sponsored "eye-opener" visits to some of the poorer and rougher areas of the nearby city. These "eye-openers" were designed by several self-described "closet liberals" who hoped to expand the religious vision of St. Andrew's privileged youth. The "eye-openers," however, encouraged the decoding of another, more powerful message—that is, while the dominant culture blessed those who work hard, it also "had a bad and dangerous edge" (conference tape, p. 7). If you do not work hard, this message implies, you can "fall off" (conference tape, p. 7). Such "eye-openers" into the underclass areas seemed to confirm the message that "you needed to keep your nose to the grindstone, work hard, get to college and work even harder" (conference tape, p. 7). Thus, the short drive from an urban ghetto to Crestwood lifted up "how good the culture was to those who lived in Crestwood" (conference tape, p. 7).

In response to this dilemma, I am drawn to the story of Anne, the St. Andrew's peer ministry staffer who quit the staff because she had to get into a good school:

> [She realized] that she had a good life now and also realized that she would have a hard time maintaining that lifestyle on her own. She also realized that it was a stressful pursuit but didn't know any better direction and also didn't have confidence that she could attain such an economic level for herself. She was in a double-bind. If anything the "eye-opener" showed her why she had to stay on the ladder. If she didn't achieve success, go to college, continue to compete, she would "fall off the ladder" and be lost—wind up like those people she saw in the city. [conference tape, p. 7]

Thus, while a caring St. Andrew's adult organized the "eye-openers" in order to expand each youth's vision, the exact opposite occurred. The youth's horizon closed down: "The shadow-side of this idea was that it reemphasized how bad it is to fail and how necessary it is to compete. It reinforced the idea that salvation means 'being safe'; i.e., you must be a 'success'" (conference tape, p. 7).

An observation was made by one youth pastor regarding this kind of stress: "Such a double-bind situation as the one this girl experienced is the type of situation that contributes to teen suicide. It is a 'catch-22' situation; the kids experience pressure to be successful, but in addition they state they will never be as much of a success as their parents have been (because it takes so much more now to succeed) so they feel doomed to failure" (conference tape, p. 7).

A model (like this corporation model with its emphasis on the educative ladder), once established, stubbornly resists change. Such a model indicates the *embedded* structures that make up the interpretive patterns of an organization. At St. Andrew's the introduction of other models threatens the embedded model. The corporation model becomes "the way we do things at St. Andrew's." Other models are risky; they are not tolerated. The ragged edges around the corporation model at St. Andrew's indicate there *are* other models present that have different implications; for example: the laity refusing to hire a "director of youth program" in favor of an ordained minister could mean that they define "ministry" as religiously more complex than the direction of a set of "educative programs." The weight, however, of the embedded model prevents this ragged edge from tearing the whole cloth.

Given St. Andrew's understanding of the church, we should not be surprised that Jack, operating out of a different set of symbols and signs, after roughly two and a half years of service, "burned out." Barbara Wheeler, commenting on the church's adoption of the corporation "systems" approach for professional management, notes:

Systems tend to use up their leaders. In the systems image of an organization leaders are simply instruments for getting the job done. If the instrument wears out, you replace it, since it has no intrinsic but only instrumental value to the system. This view of people as dispensable, replaceable parts makes leadership jobs in systems difficult, and risky. Corporations compensate their managers for the risk and impersonality of their jobs by paying huge salaries. Ministers, too, must constantly prove their instrumental worth, and thus like managers they are in difficult and risky positions, always in danger of wearing out, or malfunctioning, and being disposed of. Unlike corporate managers, though, they do not have cushions like large salaries and stock options. No wonder we have a problem with what has come to be called "clergy burnout." There is no security in the role; there is constant pressure on the job; there is no financial security if things go wrong. Many people cannot survive long with that much uncertainty.[30]

PART TWO

YOUTH MINISTRY AND THE QUESTIONING OF CULTURE

Chapter 5 presents a historical overview of the development of the black church in America, while chapters 6 through 8 describe youth ministry in one specific context: Grace Church, a large, African-American, middle-class, United Church of Christ congregation located in the urban midwest.

While no two African-American congregations are exactly alike, Grace Church enjoys the reputation of being a solid and consistent example of what "good" youth ministry looks like in a mainstream denominational congregation that is black.

With later chapters (chapters 9 and 10) offering a sharper focus on how Grace Church illustrates "black style" youth ministry, chapter 6 (class, kinship, and youth ministry) emphasizes the power of a "kinship" model of youth ministry at Grace Church. Chapter 7 ("A Black Context: Grace Church") points out how the religious existence of Grace Church is a challenge to the dominant culture.

Through such historical grounding, description, and analysis of one specific African-American context, chapters 5 through 8 suggest that "black style" youth ministries (like Grace Church's) have always embodied a critical stance toward American culture, and are therefore sharply aware of the alternative religious roles faith communities take to prevent being swallowed by dominant culture.

By its explicit rejection of America's dominant cultural ethos, the youth ministry emphasis of a congregation like Grace Church serves as a religious catechetical program, always in tension with the values of the dominant culture.

CHAPTER
FIVE

DANGEROUS LISTENING: WHITES, BLACKS, AND SLAVERY

Dangerous listening . . . is a form of listening in which previously unheard voices break through to the centerpoint of our lives and reveal new and dangerous insights for the present. Such listening illuminates for a few moments and with a harsh steady light the questionable nature of things we have apparently come to terms with and shows up the banality of too much of our ministry.

Maria Harris[1]

Immersed in the interpretive tasks of adolescence, contemporary Anglo and African-American persons of faith inherit the racial mindsets and ecclesiastical patterns that often burden the present with the bigotries and the crippling social structures developed in the past. No period of history is more important, given the concerns of this book, than 1600 to 1900. Uncovering a few of the shifting and often disturbing events within this time frame encourages us to ask in what measure the feelings, patterns, and expectations connected with these historical moments continue to exist today, and what we might make of them.

Indentured Servitude and Economic Priorities

As part of a Dutchman's cargo, in 1619 the first Africans arrived in Virginia, and were contracted to the Jamestown colonists as indentured servants. These blacks joined other indentured whites and native Americans, contracted for specific periods of servitude as based upon English apprenticeship and vagrancy laws.[2] With indentured servitude as a key link in the English court system, the colonies became a dumping ground for Europe's unwanted poor, criminal, idle, and wretched. Such "undesirables" often received sentences of "'transportation' and seven years exile in the colonies."[3] Adventurers outside the court system often voluntarily contracted themselves into indentured servanthood for passage to the free world. While most indentured servants were English or Dutch, others seeking passage to the colonies came from the remaining north European countries. In addition, many unfortunates including families were waylaid and captured from the streets of cities and towns, "spirited" away into indentured servanthood.

Indentured servanthood was not an easy passage—the trade in Irish servants was so nasty that it became known as "the Irish Slave Trade."[4] Often, families were broken up, with children under five "sold or given away until their twenty-first birthday."[5] As Lerone Bennett Jr. notes:

> The very important point here is that both black and white bondage grew out of and reflected the internal tensions of Europe. These tensions revolved around certain ideas about the proper subordination of white people, and a new milieu of competitive egoism growing out of the Renaissance and the Commercial Revolution. And out of this there finally emerged a new spirit of adventure and ruthlessness that included a certain contempt for all human beings and a willingness to use any and every expedient in the search for gold, glory, and conquests for God.[6]

Consequently, indentured servitude constituted the economic labor base for the colonies, and the bulk of indentured servants were white: "Whatever the form, whatever the style, white servitude was a system designed to extract the maximum amount of labor power from poor whites."[7] At least eighty thousand indentured servants arrived in Virginia alone during the colonial period.[8] As Joseph R. Washington Jr. reminds us: "Jamestown was not an experiment in religious freedom, but in free enterprise."[9]

E. Franklin Frazier suggests that "the original twenty Negroes were freed after seven years of indentured labour and that at least one among them, an Anthony Johnson, acquired considerable land after becoming free."[10] As indentured servants, sharing "what can only be called equality of oppression, blacks fared about as well as whites. Many black servants, like many white servants, worked for a specified number of years and were freed. Some blacks served longer terms than most whites, but some blacks also served shorter terms than the four-to-seven years required of most whites."[11] Routinely "bound out" as contracted servants, blacks and whites alike completed their terms, came to own land, to vote, and to actively participate in the freedom of public life.

Over the next fifty to one hundred years, this system of indenturing black and white servants yielded to the emerging institution of slavery. In that time, a number of factors coalesced, making slavery the option preferred over the indenturing of captured Africans: (1) slavery came to be seen as a better economic bargain than the relatively short-term use of indentured servants; (2) the slave supply, actively supported by the formation in 1672 of Great Britain's *Royal African Company*, seemed inexhaustible; (3) Africans were thought to work better than whites with hot-climate crops; and (4) Africans were easily identifiable and were without power in a white country.

After 1640, captured Africans who at one time would have been contracted with for set periods of indentured servitude began to be viewed as "permanent" servants, sold without benefit of contract. While slavery was still illegal in Massachusetts in 1641, Africans "lawfully captured" could be sold as slaves in the marketplace. This was an economic measure to provide an adequate labor force. Such a measure required religious arguments for justification, but "Negroes were [said to be] a cursed people, and enslavement was [therefore] a proper method to bring them within the reach of God's grace."[12]

The Role of White Religion in Slavery

Religion played a key role in the emerging institution of slavery. Indeed, in the seventeenth century, "a professional education in the law, the ministry, or medicine was one of the surest avenues into the slaveholding class."[13] This was to remain true until the Civil War.[14] As Christian ministers came to own slaves, they became adept in defending slavery through the use of elaborate doctrinal statements and the "authority" of the Bible. With rare exception, slave owners and whites in general "took the political orthodoxy of their ministers increasingly for granted and came to regard them as supporters of the plantation social order."[15]

The earliest efforts to convert slaves came from those priests who initially accompanied the Virginia planters. They felt, as a matter of course, that slaves ought to be baptized. This action seemed destined to set them at odds with the planters. The planters believed *freedom* and *Christianity* to be inseparable ideas; if baptism indeed implied freedom, then slave owners had a distinct problem. Those thousands of cheaply purchased slaves would necessarily revert to indentured status, a status guaranteeing eventual freedom. But if this option caused revulsion among slave owners, "the other possibility was equally repulsive. The conversion of slaves to Christianity and their baptism would require their being set free immediately as real human persons, potential brothers, entitled to be respected as sacred men and women."[16]

Pragmatically, in order to maintain access to the black slaves for the purpose of baptism, the religious authorities agreed to a resolution that solved both sides of the quandary. In 1667, for example, the Christians of Virginia determined that blacks could actively be evangelized as long as it was understood that "Baptism doth not alter the condition of the person as to his bondage or freedom; in order that diverse masters freed from this doubt may more carefully endeavor the propagation of Christianity."[17] The seeds were planted; on this basis slave owners would permit baptism even as the church dissociated Christianity from freedom. John Hope Franklin notes:

> Gradually the doctrine that freedom was inherent in Christianity began to wane in popularity and was supplanted by a point of view that was in itself a rationalization of the institution. This view was that slavery was good in that it brought heathens into contact with Christianity and led to the salvation of their souls.[18]

Concurrent with such accommodations on the part of the church, racist theories regarding the inferiority of blacks and the natural superiority of whites became ascendant, with the end result being the destruction of black legal rights. "To put the matter simply, and rather bluntly, slavery was designed to turn human beings into machines."[19] Eventually, "slave codes" came into effect:

> It was a crime ... for a slave to read and write. It was a crime, punishable by a summary lashing, for an African to stand up straight and look a white man in the eye. It was a crime for slaves to hold meetings or religious services without a white witness. Slaves could not congregate in groups of more than two or three away from the home plantations. They could not beat drums, wear fine clothes, or carry sticks or weapons. They could not marry, they could not protect their children or their mates.[20]

The impact was felt by blacks and whites alike. It became "very expensive for a white person to like black people or to love them. This was not, it should be emphasized, a matter of hints and vague threats. The laws were quite explicit."[21]

Evangelism and Conversion

In 1726 evangelical revivals in Europe became "the Great Awakening" in the colonies. In *Slave Religion*, Albert J. Raboteau suggests that during these years "blacks were among those lifted to new heights of religious excitement."[22] In the midst of revival meetings, the argument over whether or not blacks had souls ended. Emmanuel L. McCall points out that when slaves began to be included in the camp meetings, "without seeking permission or further discussion, the slaves were experiencing the same emotional manifestations of their masters. Mass conversions occurred among the slave population. This prompted the need for continuing worship opportunities."[23] Until 1790, colonial religion was marked by this new style of "rough-hewn frontier preaching."[24] Blacks responded, "and were, for the most part, welcomed as participants."[25]

The Methodists and Baptists, architects of this revival process, were "vehement against slavery during those first years following the Revolutionary War."[26] They were also in the forefront in evangelization practices among the black slaves.[27] Raboteau assesses the impact of such evangelism upon local congregations:

> In 1786, the first year in which Methodists distinguished white and black members in their records, there were 1,890 black members out of a total membership of 18,791. By 1790 the number of black Methodists had increased to 11,682, and in 1797 the black membership stood at 12,215, or almost one-fourth of the total Methodist membership. The majority of black Methodists in 1797 were located in three states: Maryland, with 5,106; Virginia, with 2,490; and North Carolina, with 2,071. South Carolina followed with 890, while Georgia had 148.

Unlike the Methodists, Baptists kept sparse records, so it is difficult to gauge accurately the extent of their black membership, particularly during the early period of their expansion. One estimate is that in 1793 the black Baptist membership was about one-fourth the total membership of 73,471, or between 18,000 and 19,000.[28]

There was an explosion of new congregations, with the circuit rider well suited "to the needs and conditions of the rural South."[29] An emphasis upon *conversion* instead of education became a leveling influence among clergy and laity as well as blacks and whites; indeed, both Methodists and Baptists encouraged religious fervor and an ability to "preach the word" as more important than a well-educated clergy. Raboteau provides numerous examples of black preachers who, from the 1760s into the 1800s, preached with fervor in black, white, and mixed congregations.[30]

Nevertheless, while blacks were active in these Methodist and Baptist meetings (blacks preached and had numerous followers who were black and white[31]), as slaves they were prohibited by custom and by law from establishing organizations, including churches, without the presence of the master or of a representative from the ruling class.[32] As a result, southern blacks regularly were coerced to attend the religious services of their masters.[33] With the rise of the "cotton kingdom" and the increased demand for slaves after 1815, Methodist and Baptist evangelicals were able "to dismiss their radical beginnings [with their anti-slavery pronouncements] and concentrate upon the regeneration of society through the regeneration of each individual."[34]

A New Reality

Taken primarily from the west coast of Africa, these enslaved Africans represented numerous tribal groupings, spoke a variety of languages, and reflected differing understandings of the African worldview. Nevertheless, they shared similar "ideas about social organization and the nature of the forces that controlled the world."[35] Severed from Africa by slavery, the social basis of the African religious life in America had disintegrated "as a coherent system of belief. From the moment they arrived in America and began to toil as slaves, they could not help absorbing the religion of the master class."[36] Still, they "overtly, covertly, and even intuitively fought" to shape their religious life themselves.[37]

Eugene D. Genovese suggests that "the religion of the slaves manifested many African 'traits' and exhibited greater continuity with African ideas than has generally been appreciated. But it reflected a different reality in a vastly different land and in the end emerged as something new."[38] Traditional West African religion provided Africans with an integrated worldview, in which "religion was an aspect, not a feature, of society . . . the vital way in which the entire human body collectively expressed its essence."[39] Traditional religion also bequeathed to African Americans "a vision of being debtors to the ages and, accordingly, a sense of responsibility to those who came before."[40] Elders were respected. "African tradition [also] imparted to the religion of the slaves an irrepressible affirmation of life—an ability to see the world as a 'vale of tears' and yet experience a joy in life that has sometimes evoked admiration from whites, sometimes contempt, but almost always astonishment."[41]

The presence of such traditional African religious values transformed and changed antebellum black Christianity into a new thing, by infusing it with African-oriented melodies and rhythms, and by adding new features, such as the ring shout, ecstatic seizure, and communal, call-and-response participation.[42] Because such a merger and such a new thing, given the planters' concerns with slavery, Christianity, and freedom, was unsettling to the slaveholder class, the slaves created "a vast invisible structure of worship, which differed materially from the visible and oppressive services ('Slaves be obedient to your masters') of the whites."[43] In this process, Genovese argues that the fiery style and the uninhibited emotionalism of the revival-centered Methodist and Baptist preachers exerted a tremendous appeal to these transplanted Africans. Thus, "the insistence that the community worship God in a way that integrated the various forms of human expression—song, dance, and prayer, all with call-and-response, as parts of a single offering the beauty of which pays homage to God."[44]

The masters held the slaves' religion in contempt, for in truth they feared it. Genovese notes that such fear was based on the fact that "the slaves had achieved a degree of psychological and cultural autonomy and therefore had successfully resisted becoming extensions of their masters' wills—the one thing they were supposed to become."[45] The merger of this "invisible institution" following the Civil War into the independent black church organizations "provided an organization and structuring of Negro life which has persisted until the present time."[46]

Resistance to Slavery

Thus the lines were drawn and the splitting of America into black and white begun. Certainly there was visible resistance from both blacks and whites. Raboteau suggests that "as early as 1774 American slaves were declaring publicly and politically that they thought Christianity and slavery were incompatible."[47] Slave resistance took many forms; some slaves escaped to the north while others subverted their masters' desires. Raboteau comments: "Lying and deceit, normally considered moral vices, were virtues to slaves in their dealings with whites."[48] Still others resorted to violence.

Religion played a key role in all forms of resistance. For example, Nat Turner, a Baptist "exhorter" and a visionary who believed that the Bible offered a solution for slavery, killed fifty-five whites with his band of ex-slaves before being captured and hanged. The "Nat Turner Revolt" of 1831 struck terror in the hearts of slave owners. While Turner was deeply religious, and seemingly not a good example of the dominant thesis that Christianity promoted social control among slaves, slaves *without* religion seemed even more frightening. The resulting ambivalence led to a peculiar juxtapositioning of practices; during this period, for example, laws were passed against slaves reading, writing, and preaching. At the same time there was great "encouragement of oral instruction of slaves in the Christian faith, and campaigns to encourage more humane treatment of slaves."[49] As slave holders more self-consciously embraced religion within a proslavery stance, they "increasingly paid white preachers to conduct services for their slaves."[50] Some slave holders went so far as to build chapels, or "praise-houses" for the slaves.[51]

In all of this, the slave owners' motives were mixed. Some assumed religion was only a pragmatic means for controlling slaves, yet others who held differing opinions would not try to eliminate black preaching. "Some had the good sense to know that if the slaves were listening to a reliable white preacher, they could not—not that moment, at any rate—be off in the woods listening to some suspect black exhorter."[52] After 1831, the southern churches were unified on the issue of slavery—they "either grudgingly accepted the facts of life or warmly embraced the proslavery argument, [putting] themselves in a position to proselytize among the slaves with the blessings and active support of the masters."[53]

Northern Congregations

In the north, while slavery had been abolished, most denominations implicitly accepted racist principles, allowing slave owners, for example, to remain in congregations as full members even after their parent denominations had split along northern/southern lines. As late as 1861, the General Assembly of the Presbyterian Church declared "that the slave system had generally proven "kindly and benevolent" and had provided "real effective discipline" to a people who could not be elevated in any other way. Slavery, it concluded, was the black man's "normal condition."[54] Some northern congregations wrote statements affirming that slavery was a secular issue outside church concern. Others had long debates concerning this issue.

No major denomination, prior to the Civil War, advocated immediate emancipation.[55] Indeed, while early abolitionists had felt confident in recruiting clergy to join the antislavery cause, they quickly discovered that there was little or no support from these ranks. The clergy flatly shied away from such controversial involvement.[56] "All but a few small denominations balked at a commitment to uncompromised abolitionist principles and programs."[57] Abolitionists "accused religious institutions of thwarting rather than promoting God's will."[58] Black and white abolitionists sought, but did not receive, a clear-cut repudiation of slavery. Nevertheless, the abolitionist debate, with all its internal factions and issues, "contributed to moving the churches closer to abolitionist principles and practices by the coming of the Civil War."[59]

The Rise of Separate Black Congregations

During the late eighteenth century black and white abolitionists, the Underground Railroad, and the heady atmosphere of the Revolutionary War combined to substantially increase the number of free African Americans in the north. This accomplishment, however, resulted in a mixed reception. While a few blacks were acceptable in most northern congregations, Genovese notes that hostile whites were very willing to direct blacks into separate churches. He also suggests that blacks often greeted denominational divisions with enthusiasm, "partly because they felt uncomfortable and wished to practice their religion in their own way, and partly because they resented the inferior position into which they were being thrust within the white churches."[60] Northern Anglo Americans, when the opportunity for openness was visibly apparent, instead accepted the racial rhetoric concerning African Americans, and denied ecclesiastical equality to blacks.

Lawrence Jones provides an apt summary of the contemporaneous practices in late eighteenth-century white, northern churches:

> Blacks were, more often than not, second-class citizens in the predominantly white churches to which they belonged. It was common practice for pews to be provided for them in reserved sections of the churches. These benches were conventionally referred to as "nigger pews." In some churches blacks could only commune after the whites had done so; in others they could not vote or serve in any official capacity. Segregated sections for blacks were provided in church cemeteries so that the moldering dust of blacks and whites might not become mingled, even after death. Not every congregation followed every one of these discriminatory practices, but no major Protestant body was free from some taint of racist thought and practice.[61]

While the reasons for the rise of separate black congregations are complex, one argument asserts that most of these congregations were responses to the racism of white congregations.[62] For example, Richard Allen, arguably the most well-known late eighteenth-century black preacher, was instrumental in making a visible break with white custom. Allen was born a slave in Philadelphia and purchased his freedom in 1777 from a slave owner "who was receptive to the freedom movement, and in the same year he was converted by Methodist preachers. Three years later

Allen was preaching. His talents as a preacher came to the attention of Bishop Asbury, who gave him assignments and allowed him to travel with white ministers."[63]

E. Franklin Frazier tells the story:

> [When Richard Allen] went to Philadelphia in 1786 he was invited to preach in the St. George Methodist Episcopal Church. When Allen observed in Philadelphia the need of the Negroes for religious leadership and an organization, he proposed that a separate church be established for Negroes. His proposal was opposed both by whites and Negroes. However, when the number of Negroes attending St. George Methodist Episcopal Church increased, Negroes were removed from the seats around the wall and ordered to sit in the gallery. Mistaking the section of the gallery which they were to occupy, Allen, Absalom Jones, and another member were almost dragged from their knees as they prayed. They left the church and together with other Negro members founded the Free African Society.[64]

The Free African Society was not a church, but a visible vehicle for African-American protest. Joseph R. Washington Jr. notes that "it became the major vehicle for deciding where and how Negroes should worship."[65] Of major interest is the choice by these men of the term *African*. Allen hoped to form a separate church on race, though based on Methodist principles. He became the pioneer bishop of the African Methodist Episcopal Church. Allen's friend, Absalom Jones, felt that the Methodists discriminated against blacks, and therefore "organized the St. Thomas African Protestant Episcopal Church, and became the P.E.C.'s first Negro priest."[66] By 1812 "there were black churches of every conceivable description."[67] Black clergy "were in the vanguard of the anti-slavery and abolitionist movements."[68] By the time of the Civil War, free black churches "had grown and expanded the territories within which they exercised jurisdiction."[69] They quickly became "the most substantial institution and the largest owner of property in the black communities."[70]

Out of this period of African-American history came a black culture characterized by an ethos of mutuality. In part, blacks had removed themselves from white congregations because they felt insufficient concern on the part of whites "for the souls of their kin," and because of inadequate attention being paid to the stressful conditions in which many African Americans now found themselves.

CHAPTER SIX

CLASS, KINSHIP, AND YOUTH MINISTRY

The dominant culture's denigrations of the black family
system come out of white America's romance with rugged
individualism. To the conqueror of the plains and the
subjugator of the Native American, a man's man was
someone who took care of his family first, asked for no help
and was up to whatever violence was necessary to insure
that self and family dignity were not violated.

Wallace Charles Smith[1]

Grace Church, the African-American church of this
study, encourages its adolescents to become involved in the
leadership (through song, scripture, prayer, *and sermon*) of
the Sunday celebration of worship held every fifth Sunday.
On one such Sunday a young woman named Roberta
brought the message. Reflecting on the problems facing
King Ahab and his need for good advice (1 Kings 21), this
high school senior noted how King Ahab's four hundred
resident prophets were employed as "permanent religious
advisors." Roberta suggested that these advisors had
"developed an agenda" to keep their privileged positions—
"they told the King exactly what he wanted to hear" (tape R,
p. 1). She continued, "Here we have four hundred prophets, all worried about keeping their jobs, holding those
influence-producing long lunches, staying on the King's
good side, and getting promoted; they *had their own agenda*"
(tape R, p. 1). She then warned, "We should beware of

people who have their own agendas" (tape R, p. 1). Reflecting further, Roberta stated, for example: "Some of today's educators comprise a myopic minority, a group who have internalized a completely Euro-centric world view and who look on anything African with suspicion and disgust" (tape R, p. 2).

"As students spending a great deal of their time in school," Roberta suggested, "we often hear this myopic minority asserting that everything European is of value while everything African is worthless. These teachers, while not the majority, are nonetheless like that teacher who told Malcolm X, when he was a young and a smart student, 'A smart nigger like you should study carpentry, not law'" (tape R, p. 2). Roberta concluded: "Folk like Malcolm X's teacher mutilate our mentality and pervert our personality. Either they don't care, don't want to make waves, or are so brainwashed that they believe the racist lies they perpetuate upon our youth. Whatever the reason, they steal our education from us and turn us out of schools ready to serve the needs of the military-industrial system. Beware, Grace Church, of folk like these teachers—a myopic minority— who *have their own agendas*" (tape R, p. 12).

Roberta's sermon directly challenges St. Andrew's "myth of origin," the ongoing interpretive story of their causal past, an interpretive story centered upon those fierce and rugged Anglo-American individuals who "made it" on the risky frontier of our ever-expanding society. In contrast, Roberta and Grace Church understand their formative story as being centered in a spirit-filled, oppressed people, African Americans who survived, with God's help, by caring for one another. St. Andrew's "agenda" rests in the dynamics of competition, while Grace's resides in the dynamics of mutual sharing. While the metaphors concerning "church" that might emerge from such differing agendas are diverse, it is not surprising that St. Andrew's regards its organization as a figurative *corporation* and that

Grace figuratively describes "church" as a politically aware and spiritually alive *kinship system*.

Kinship

In *The Church in the Life of the Black Family*, Wallace Charles Smith suggests that historically the black church supported blacks at society's breakpoints. He notes that the black church was born from West African concepts of extended family and kinship, which could not evade the implications of parents and children consistently being "sold away at the masters' whims."[2] For Smith, the black church grew and "evolved as a new family for those who were continually being uprooted from their original families."[3] Smith indicates the core of that African-American church can be understood only by reference to the kinship network as it flexibly emerged in the American context. Smith argues that the black family was able to survive slavery because of "its adaptability to change and its extended (rather than nuclear) structure."[4] Kinship adapted to the conditions of slavery was not the same as it was in Africa; nevertheless, kinship under slavery became a key concept for the black family and its extension, the black church.

When newly arrived African slaves entered the emerging slave culture, family ties were established using kinship as the organizing methodology. Despite the oppressive conditions of slavery, such kinship networks flourished.[5] Within such networks, the naming of individuals provided cues as to the significance attached to such "kin" groupings. Children, for example, frequently were named for persons outside the immediate family. In addition, older slaves unrelated by blood or marriage frequently were honored with the names of "aunt" or "uncle." This was part of an intentional "fictive kin" process: "making children address all adult blacks as either 'aunt' or 'uncle' socialized them into the enlarged slave community and also invested non-kin slave relationships with symbolic kin meanings and functions."[6] Speaking from a contemporary perspective, one author notes: "While broadly applied family terms like 'Brother,' 'Sister,' 'members,' 'bloods,' and 'Cuz' may seem strange and confusing to outsiders, they are quite familiar and reasonable to Afro-Americans. They have been in use in the Black community for generations."[7] In addition, surnames kept by slaves served to shape a social identity independent of slave ownership, and were rarely the surname of a slave's final owner.[8]

In all of this, there was a drive by blacks to define a kinship network in ways that symbolically separated slaves from slave owners. "To understand, as the slaves did, that at any moment a spouse, a sister, a brother, a mother, or a father could be sold and never be seen or heard of again made family ties even more precious."[9] Family ties meant free slaves would risk everything in order to free a family member. Family ties meant not escaping even if the chance were offered. Family ties meant slaves who had escaped into semifreedom, working for years in order to purchase those kin who were still enslaved. Such practices bound blacks to one another while infusing the community with broad conceptions of obligation. Within such an extended conception of community, "A teen-ager sold from the Upper to the lower South after 1815 was cut off from his or her immediate Upper South family, but found many fictive aunts and uncles in the Lower South."[10]

These conceptions anchored the task of caring and socializing children, furthered racial solidarity, and spiritually ordered a community that regularly had been disordered by the whims of slave owners. Kin networks and their attendant practices seemed to affirm that if you hurt someone in the "family," you hurt everyone. Indeed, during and following the Civil War, parentless children regularly were absorbed by such "fictive" kinship networks.[11] In effect, by the time of the Civil War, the West African kin structures "had been transformed by the slaves themselves into larger social and communal obligations. These were the beliefs of men who addressed each other as 'Uncle,' not 'Mister.'"[12]

Phenomenologically, the black church in America grew from these roots. With emancipation, the black kinship network continued to be a key part of the growing black churches. During Reconstruction African-American denominations were immersed in the enormous problems of those newly "freed." "This was assumed to be a temporary need and the folk anticipated the day when the preacher and the fellowship would bring about freedom and equality."[13] But with the resumption of segregation in the south and discrimination in the north, the militancy of the freed black in this regard was curbed. Nevertheless, urban and rural studies indicate that at the turn of the century the black helping tradition was still alive and well.[14] Institutionalized through the rise of racial uplift organizations and still powerful within black congregations, the kinship helping concept continued to play a dominant role in both the black extended family and the black church.

As African Americans moved north, the black church functioned, in part to make the city smaller and more manageable, but "for the first time in Afro-American history, the helping tradition was not required for black people to survive."[15] Blacks could "make it" on their own, as individuals, in the big city. The size of the cities and the variety of opportunities, while not particularly good in comparison to white possibilities, eliminated the absolute necessity for the helping tradition. As both the helping tradition and the movement toward freedom waned, Frazier saw the black church in retreat, becoming "a refuge in a hostile white world."[16]

James P. Comer, in commenting on his own coming of age, notes that the black church came to function as a "substitute culture."[17] Comer continues: "Education and opportunities in the 'outside world' enabled some to keep their feet in two cultures—the church and the total society. Others, for various reasons, remained enmeshed in the culture of the church alone."[18] Comer would agree with Frazier's comment that the black church provided "a means of catharsis for . . . pent-up emotions and frustrations."[19] Comer, noting the intensity of emotion exhibited within the black church, observed that while some African and southern black and white religious elements were no doubt present, "the intensity of the response reflected the sense of frustration and helplessness the people felt. The church was the place to discharge frustration and hostility so that one could face injustice and hardship the rest of the week."[20]

In 1964 Joseph Washington Jr. expressed his considerable anger at the inward turning of the black kinship helping tradition and those ministers who had also turned their backs on the struggle for justice. For Washington, the church ought to be the meeting place where blacks pursue their "primary business: working together to pursue and achieve equal rights and opportunity for each and all."[21] As the radical nature of the helping tradition eroded, Washington's assessment was bitter: "As an agency in accommodating the Negro to his [sic] subordinate role in society, the Negro congregation was without a peer."[22]

A sharp critique of the current status of the black helping tradition by Joanne and Elmer Martin argues that the black helping tradition "began to decline rapidly during the 1930s and has sunk nearly into insignificance today."[23] Written in 1985, *The Helping Tradition In the Black Family and Community* by the Martins argues that both a "street ethic" and a middle-class "get your own" mentality has radically revisioned the core of the black kinship understanding of life. While these authors optimistically see an awareness of the positive implications of black culture and a potential refocusing of the kinship network as avenues to revitalize the black helping tradition, they suggest that "the helping tradition in the urban black community is being supplanted by the bourgeoisie and street ideologies."[24]

In an earlier book, *The Black Extended Family*, the Martins indicated that urban blacks were heading "home" to the south: "Few extended family members write 'home' anymore telling family members about the 'bright lights' and opportunities of the city.... Others are eager to follow—still in search of the promised land"[25] In part, the Martins suggest, this reverse migration is tied to the emptiness and an absence of the helping tradition in the urban style of life. They conclude:

> The fictive kinship, racial consciousness, and religious consciousness necessary for transferring the major values of the extended family to the wider community have, for the most part, been checked by the individualistic, dog-eat-dog, competitive orientation of the dominant urban society.[26]

The New Black Middle Class

In a paper given at a consultation on "ministries to black youth," Romney M. Moseley indicated his suspicion that "black churches are caught up in the effort to become more middle class and that the success of middle class blacks is becoming the dominant ideology for the identity formation and leadership development of black youth."[27] Despite arguments over definitions regarding "blacks who are/are not *middle class*," it can be asserted that as a result of a booming economy and the civil rights movement of the 1960s, a "new" black middle class emerged, doubling in size and "encompassing 27 percent of all black workers by 1970."

While this enlarged, first-generation, black middle class emerged in the 1960s, during the 1970s it slowed in growth because of severe economic conditions—that is, "without prosperity, the civil rights laws lost much of their impact."[29] Nevertheless, expectations in this nation had changed: blacks in the "middle class" now might expect to be accountants, consultants, middle-range executives, engineers, or elected officials. No longer were "middle-class" blacks drawn exclusively from the ministry, education, funeral business, postal service, law, or medicine. "For a variety of reasons, then, it was appropriate to speak of a *new* black middle class by 1970."[30]

Despite such advances, it can be argued that the experience of today's "first-generation" black middle class "remains separate and substantially different from that of the white middle class."[31] Uncertainty concerning how "new" middle-class blacks get treated indicates that the "black middle class still seems more to be poised on the banks of the mainstream than to be swimming in its current."[32] Members of the new black middle class have difficulty believing they "belong." They assume the old "two-world" mentality of race still holds true—in one world they are accepted for themselves while in the other world race still comes first.

The suspicion by blacks that they are not fully "allowed" into the dominant culture is well founded. In the first national study comparing residential segregation patterns for blacks, Hispanics, and Asians, University of Chicago researchers Nancy Denton and Douglas Massey reported in 1989 that "even when blacks raise their education and income levels, they consistently are unable to find housing in integrated neighborhoods"[33] Being interviewed regarding the research report, Denton indicated that the fundamental cleavage seems to be between blacks and nonblacks. She explained that middle-class blacks cannot live in the same quality neighborhoods as whites with similar backgrounds. This translates into blacks—whatever class—experiencing worse housing, poorer education, higher death rates, and higher crime rates than whites. Denton and Massey conclude that "the American dream of 'working one's way up' is not a viable option for blacks in the United States, at least in terms of residence."[34]

Whenever a middle-class black "succeeds," and moves out of what Denton and Massey describe as "poorer quality neighborhoods," the downside to that mobility is inner-city destabilization, says University of Chicago sociologist William Julius Wilson. His recent work emphasizes the role of "class" and the role of middle-class black families in anchoring urban neighborhoods. When such families pursue their rising class expectations, Wilson suggests the resulting black flight disastrously impacts the urban ghetto.[35] Therefore, even while a segment of the African-American population is successfully competing with Anglo Americans, it is the peculiar institution of American racism that promotes segregated patterns of living and the resultant isolation of what some have called an "underclass."

Reporting in March 1989, the House Ways and Means Committee indicated that the "rich" in this country indeed were getting richer, while the "poor" were getting poorer: from 1979 to 1987 the average household income of the poorest fifth fell 6.1 percent, while the richest rose 11.1 percent. If we commence those figures with the years 1973 to 1978 the gap grows larger—11.8 percent loss for the poorest fifth; 24.1 percent gain for the already wealthy.[36] Upon hearing these figures writer James Lardner suggests: "We have begun to entertain the idea that severe and lasting material differences among people—a class system, in short—is the natural condition of humanity. Already, nearly half the American people have no adult memory of a time when income inequality was declining."[37]

Nevertheless, the power of the dominant culture is such that, in the words of Joanne and Elmer Martin, "the overall desire of blacks to raise their individual social class status takes priority over uplifting the entire race."[38] Indeed, these authors believe the individualistic adaptations of contemporary African Americans to the competitive nature of the dominant culture are primarily focused on "getting ahead"—that is, blacks are no different from whites in this respect. They "are merely following the individualistic dictates to which all Americans are subjected. Thus, following consistently the norms of their society, these blacks are not required to, and are even encouraged not to, concern themselves with anybody but themselves."[39] In the absence of an effective African-American helping/kinship tradition, "many social scientists studying ghetto life have come to see the street ideology and the cool lifestyle as the authentic black culture."[40] The Martins counter with their argument that "the street ideology is deviant from—the very antithesis of—legitimate black culture."[41] Nevertheless, such street ideologies are highly persuasive for contemporary youth.

In an essay entitled "Ethnic Identity, Development, and Black Expressiveness," Geneva Gay argues that "a positive, healthy perception of ethnic identity is not an automatic birthright for most Blacks."[42] Her affirmation, in light of this potential misperception by many blacks, is that all blacks need "ethnic actualization."[43] This is not an automatic process. She suggests: As black children "become mature enough to understand symbolic and representational thought, their perception of Blackness changes—it becomes less subliminal and more conscious, less intuitive and more deliberate."[44] To become "ethnically actualized," however, "requires synthesizing all the pieces of [one's emerging] identity into a coherent *system* of values, attitudes, and behaviors, and then weaving them into the fabric of one's entire being. This integration is neither easy nor instantaneous."[45]

Youth Ministry as Kinship Network

Understanding this historic chain of events, Grace Church grapples with the issues of "not being white" (tape M, p. 4). "Middle-classness," in the words of one Grace Church adult, "is linked with falling away from spirituality and involves the pursuit of money, the plundering of the land, and a pseudo-identification with whites. As such, it is a pursuit doomed to failure. And it will fail, for we can never be white, and pursuing money without caring for God leads nowhere" (tape 6, p. 5). The clearest statement comes from a list of "black values" currently taught at Grace Church:

> We disavow the pursuit of *middle-classness*. . . . This classic methodology on control of captives teaches that captors must keep the captive ignorant educationally, but trained sufficiently well to serve the system. Also, the captors must be able to identify the "talented tenth" of those who show promise of providing the kind of leadership that might threaten the captor's control. Those so identified are separated from the rest of the people by: (a) structuring an economic environment that induces captive youth to fill the jails and prisons, and (b) seducing them into a socioeconomic class system which while training them to earn more dollars, hypnotizes them into believing they are better than the rest and teaches them to think in terms of "we" and "they" instead of "US"! So, while it is permissible to chase "middle-incomeness" with all our might, we must avoid the psychological entrapment of black "middle-classness." If we avoid this snare, black people no longer will be deprived of their birthright: the leadership, resourcefulness, and example of their own talented persons. [Document E, 1986]

Grace Church's Pastor Able notes "many black pastors won't address such issues with the gospel. Traditionally conservative, there still remains a strong anti-intellectual strand in the African-American community. Many of these churches try to remain the 'country church' in the big city, but we are progressive—that is, we try not to be rural; we try to be metropolitan, a black congregation with educated leadership. . . . And, from this perspective, we see the wide variety of folk needing ministry all over this city" (tape J, p. 5). Pastor Able continues, "At Grace Church there are a lot of different folk . . . a glorious mix, and we all live in the same community. But we are from both sides—those who 'have,' and those who do not. But both sides say 'we feel at home here.' We like to try and be that extended family that is progressive while also being unashamedly African-American" (tape J, p. 5).

Music provides a focus for this issue: "African Americans have been taught for a long time that church music was white music" (tape M, p. 2). What music should a progressive African-American church utilize in worship? Pastor Able responds: "So much of this is cultural. Someone says to me, 'Well, Jesus sang this one,' and I respond, 'no, he didn't; it was a German beer-drinking song and let's be clear about it,'" (tape J, p. 5). He continues: "We are products of this culture, and it's too bad when the culture says, 'This white music is sacred and the black stuff, with all the emotion and the drums, well, that's not sacred,' and we uncritically accept it. So black music has come to have a place at Grace, but not without a struggle. Grace Church's music isn't 'new,' and there is nothing wrong with 'making a joyful noise'" (tape J, p. 6).

Nevertheless, Grace Church also includes anthems from the hymnbook as regular fare: "We sing anthems—one every Sunday—intentionally. Some folk don't like this. They only want to sing spirituals. But we are hyphenated beings; we are African Americans and we've lived in this country and have a broad exposure to lots of music. So my mother loves those anthems, and we aren't going to run her out of the church because we can only sing specific songs. Now, when she comes, she sits way in the back, away from all those drums, but she comes" (tape J, p. 6).

The cutting edge of being a progressive African-American church is the issue of ordaining women as pastors. Pastor Able notes: "A lot of black churches won't ordain, and some that ordain won't hire; but some do, and more all the time. It's something I believe *must* happen" (tape J, p. 7). Roberta, the young woman preacher extensively quoted at the beginning of this chapter, "would put quite a few black male pastors I know to shame," states Pastor Able, "She knocked my socks off" (tape J, p. 2). Roberta "has the analytical tools, the language of her faith community, and a suspicion that the dominant culture may be American, but is not necessarily Christian" (tape M, p. 3).

Grace Church consistently questions "the white, dominant culture" (tape M, p. 3). By so doing, it develops caution in a too simplistic "borrowing" of that culture's models, patterns, and styles of being. Without rejecting the need for competent administrative practice, Grace Church remains wary of St. Andrew-like corporation models of youth ministry. "Such models fragment the church," indicates Pastor Able (tape J, p. 1). "When a church hires a professional youth minister to 'do' youth ministry, that youth minister has been hired to run a second church, a 'youth only church,' *alongside* the intergenerational church" (tape 6, p. 1). Pastor Able continues: "Youth in this model start relating to just the youth minister; they don't relate to the ministries and the ministers of the church. Such youth ministry tends to promote a kind of 'us' versus 'them' mentality, never the 'we' of the church; never the *belongingness*" (tape J, p. 1).

Such a model "traps" the youth minister—"youth in their late twenties who were part of such a ministry come back to see the youth minister, not to be *with* the church. Why? Because the youth program *belongs* to the youth minister. So, when kids go to college, the youth minister cries. Why set up a *private* thing like that? It's not helpful, if I'm a youth minister, when one of 'my' kids turns up bad or on drugs. Hold it. . . They aren't 'my' kids—they are the church's! We don't want to perpetuate that privatistic form of youth ministry" (tape J, p. 1).

A light sketch of Grace Church's kinship model for youth ministry centers on intergenerational, communal worship, and the empowerment of adolescents who can critique their culture from a theological African-American stance. A sponsor notes: "Every ordained minister, even Pastor Able, is intimately connected with at least one youth program" (tape 4, p. 2). Pastor Able is clear about the administrative structure of youth ministry at Grace Church: "The church has sixty ministries and each one of our five ordained ministers relates directly to twelve ministries. Roughly three of those ministries are youth-centered" (tape J, p. 2).

Youth, within this formal structure, are encouraged to run their own groups with the help of lay "sponsors"—that is, young adults and parents volunteering to provide the necessary ties. In this model, the assistant director of the Christian education committee quarterly convenes the seventeen adult "sponsors" for planning, coordination of calendar, and the solving of problems. Such a model emphasizes the supportive framework of the entire community, a "kinship network," over against the "corporation model" of youth ministry at churches like St. Andrew's.

CHAPTER
SEVEN

A BLACK CONTEXT:
GRACE CHURCH

Adult Member: Music is a very deep part of who we are. When we worship, there is a fullness of communication that surrounds and totally immerses us. But that's who we are. We respond to the spoken and sung word.

Interviewer: When I watched the children's choir, the little kids, when they rehearsed, they put in some long hours at rehearsal. And for a sizable part of that rehearsal they didn't hold any printed music; the choir leader was singing the words to them, and then they would sing, and the choir leader would sing again, then they would sing. And it was much more of an oral . . . .

Adult Member: Tradition.

Interviewer: Yeah. Rather than the printed word.

Adult Member: Right. We are a people . . . .

Interviewer: Of the oral tradition?

Adult Member: Right.

tape 1, p. 10.

Positioned in the middle of a black community of a large midwestern city on a busy street with a "Free South Africa" sign in its small front yard, Grace Church's building has a contemporary look about it. There are a number of entrances to this urban church, including ones for a preschool center and a counseling program housed within the church. Every Sunday morning finds the parking lot and the street overflowing with cars for the first of two services as eight hundred people attempt to jam themselves into a sanctuary that comfortably seats six hundred.

Entering the sanctuary, I am immediately struck by the central position of the pulpit. In front of the pulpit is a communion table covered with a white cloth. Suspended above the pulpit is a simple wooden cross. Behind the pulpit are several wooden chairs and a choir loft banked by two very bright, stained-glass windows. One side of the chancel holds a red, green, and black flag as well as an electronic organ and a piano. The other side contains a lectern and another piano. Low red brick walls on either side of the sanctuary join clear-glass upper windows and an interior beam structure running up and over a fiberglass paneled ceiling. Twelve suspended globular clusters light the sanctuary.

As I wait to be seated, I see microphones being assembled, pianos being uncovered, and musicians carrying instruments, including a set of snare drums. Four wall-mounted "Bose" speakers tilt toward the congregation; two additional speakers are positioned for the choir. The electronic organ has its own set of speakers mounted in the front corners of the sanctuary. Hidden by two of the beams is the closed-circuit video equipment used to convey this service on a twelve-foot screen in an "overflow" room where two hundred additional persons will be seated or will stand and participate in worship.

By 7:30 A.M., six blue-clad men and women have initiated the Sunday morning "devotional" with a cappella singing, "Woke Up this Morning Stayed on Jesus." During the first prayer, and every prayer thereafter, heads are bowed and hands are joined. A psalm is read, another prayer offered, the congregation sings, "Come and Go with Me," and the devotional ends.

Stacked communion trays are carried through the crowded center aisle as soft organ music and subdued conversations fill the sanctuary. Those who are going to be serving the communion gradually move toward the front cluster of pews. Lay ministers sit in the seats immediately behind the pulpit while other adults move into seats near the pulpit.

Saying "Good morning, Grace Church," an usher notes three license plates of cars with lights left on. Light laughter greets his announcement. By 7:40 the church is packed and many latecomers cannot find seats, so remain standing. I have arrived too late to be seated in the main sanctuary and therefore stand against one of the side brick walls along with more than a hundred other waiting people. Nine ushers, women dressed in white-collared blue dresses and wearing small badges on their lapels and name tags on their left pockets seat latecomers with white-gloved directions. When the sanctuary is filled, these ushers send latecomers to the overflow room and then position themselves so that they control the entrances to the side rows.

Two robed associate ministers, a woman and a man, check the microphone system while a technician takes his seat behind the piano and adjusts his earphones. This service will be broadcast on the radio, taped for shut-ins, and projected to the overflow room. The senior minister, clothed in a white robe with black doctoral stripes and black velvet piping, slowly walks down the center aisle. Behind him comes the choir, fifty strong, entering silently. There is a United Church of Christ denominational insignia visible upon the minister's robe. Stopping at the pulpit, the minister positions some notes and then sits at the electronic organ and begins to play that instrument.

By now the sanctuary has completely filled, and we remain standing on either side; unseated persons block the rear door so that I assume the overflow room is also full. Playing a steady beat on the organ while the choir director stands to lead the choir in a hand-clapping rendition of "I'm So Glad," the senior minister encourages the congregation to also stand and join in singing, which they do, slapping and keeping time to the song, which has four or five verses and which is played several times. As it is being played, one of the ushers moves those of us who have been standing along the wall into empty chairs in the choir loft. Being positioned with the choir at the front of the sanctuary enables me to see the entire congregation, which appears to be solidly black, primarily adult, middle-class, one-third male, and enthusiastically on its collective feet and singing. I note one other white person in the congregation.

As the song continues, the senior minister slides to one side of the organ bench, the choir director sits down on the other side of the bench, and without missing a beat, the senior minister stands while the choir director begins to play. By now the electronic organ, the drums and the piano are all accompanying the song, "I'm So Glad." The senior minister moves to a seat behind the central pulpit while an associate minister, dressed in a white robe, remains standing; and as the song ends, says, "We're so glad to be able to worship God today, and if you're glad, join with me in prayer." The congregation is seated, and she begins to pray. As she prays, the organist continues playing, and the choir sings, while the congregation joins in with occasional "Amens," and comments like "I'm so glad." At the conclusion of the prayer a lead singer moves the congregation into the hymn, "Holy, Holy, Holy." During this hymn (found in the hymnal in the pew rack) there is no clapping and the organ, piano, and drums quietly play in the background. By this time there is a third person sitting at the organ who continues playing while the choir director moves the congregation into a spoken/sung prayer.

This mixture of prayer and singing culminates in the singing of "The Lord's Prayer" by the entire congregation. As the choir sings, members of the congregation, in fact as many as half of the congregation, sing with the choir. When

"I'm So Glad" was sung, everyone in the congregation stood to sing with the choir; at other times, when it appears that it might only be the choir's time to sing, members of the congregation still continue to sing. And when the choir stands to sing a particular hymn, four or five members of the congregation also stand and join in, clapping and singing with the choir.

The senior minister welcomes everyone and a memory verse is shared. The pastor questions the congregation about this verse and they respond by completing each sentence he offers from the "memory verse." The pastor then names a variety of concerns he wants to have raised in prayer. Noting specific individuals who are either in or just home from the hospital, he pauses over the pain of a young man whose friend recently died from sickle-cell anemia. Another woman, home from the hospital but listed in the bulletin as being in the hospital, is also noted by the minister, who speaks about the concern of the deacons for those who are bereaved and for a new shut-in ministry to persons in pain.

Noting with some humor that there are some things that are mentioned in the bulletin that he realizes people will not read right off, the senior minister reads a letter received from denominational headquarters about globally available jobs. These jobs range from teaching English in Korea to CPA kinds of skills needed in Pakistan. Reading specific descriptions, he notes how persons from this particular church who had applied before had always found the positions filled, but that he had received the denominational letter yesterday and wanted to be quite clear that if anyone was interested in any of these particular global positions, he would speak with them after the worship service so that they could quickly contact the denomination's national office on Monday morning.

Following this discussion of shut-ins and global job possibilities, there is a "passing of the peace" during which everyone stands up, talks, shakes hands, or hugs their neighbors. Then an associate pastor asks guests to stand up; and, as the guests are standing up, the senior minister presents "pastoral care cards" to each one of the twenty-six guests. He then speaks about the current situation in South Africa and a "Song of Freedom" is performed by six black South Africans who are visiting Grace Church. After these South Africans are personally welcomed by the senior minister, he invites "all who worship with us today to partake of the Lord's Table." Moving behind the communion table, the senior and two associate pastors offer prayers of confession and forgiveness, with one pastor reciting from memory the "words from the Apostle Paul" regarding communion.

Twenty servers line up on either side of the table, face the congregation, and put on white gloves. The covered communion table is uncovered. Prayer is offered and communion trays of bread and wine are handed to each of the servers who position themselves in the aisles and begin passing the bread and wine to those seated in each pew. Recipients in the pews take a small wafer of bread and a small glass of wine, holding both until one of the ministers elevates the bread or the wine while saying, "ministering in his name, we partake of the body (blood) of Christ."

During prayer, distribution, and eating of the bread/ wine, the organ, drums, and choir continually play songs like "Spirit of the Living God." (In the service only two songs, "Holy, Holy, Holy" and "Come Thou Fount," are sung from the denominational hymnal. All others are led by the choir without hymnals.)

Communion is followed by "The Service of Giving." Ushers, including youth and children, take two collections. The first is a "general offering" taken in bucket-sized, red-lined woven baskets. The second is a "deacon benevolence offering" and is collected in light metal plates.

A "call for special prayer" at the altar results in several hundred persons rising and coming into the aisles, kneeling toward the altar, joining hands and praying while singing "Jesus Unhooked the Chains." Prayers are offered by the minister, people return to their pew seats and hear a sermon given by the senior minister on the power of God for "Living in the 'In-Between.'" Focusing the message on the "in-between" time of Acts 1:1-5, Pastor Able notes how today's time is also an "in-between" time. Like those who lived during the Acts "in-between" time, he states that we also have God's presence, power, and promise. At points during the sermon Pastor Able is almost singing, and the congregation responds with "Amens" or phrases like "Preach it, pastor."

A concluding hymn, "This Little Light of Mine," is woven into the final words of the pastor's sermon as both he and the choir exit singing with tambourines, drums, and organ playing. A benediction is given from the rear of the sanctuary (with microphone), and people immediately fill the aisles, moving toward the door where the senior minister stands, shaking hands with parishioners. Outside the church, persons hand out stewardship notes on prayer and giving. The service has taken two hours.

The Formation Process

With over five thousand members (document E, p. 9), Grace Church has acquired a large professional staff and has developed a sizable inventory of youth-oriented programs. A youth attending Grace for the first time can participate in any or all of the following age-related programs: athletes for Christ, boy scouts, building black men, building black women, church school, girl scouts, the young adult choir, or the youth fellowship.

Even with the variety and size of most of these youth-oriented programs, a coherent understanding of Grace Church's "youth ministry" is initially elusive, primarily because instead of being autonomous, each program is organized to support the centrality of Grace Church's Sunday worship experience. Indeed, Grace does not employ a professional youth minister on its staff, nor does it hold up to the congregation a special youth "department" or set of programs into which all youth are carefully placed. There seems, instead, to be an intentional evolutionary "formation" process, which gradually engages children and youth inside the language, the structures, and the worship experiences of the Grace Church faith community. Kathryn, a high school junior who is extremely active at Grace, relates how she became involved in this process:

> When I first got here I was in the "Little Warriors," you know, the children's choir. I was there until I was a freshman and then I got into the Young Adult Choir. (This is the high school youth choir.) I ushered when we weren't singing for three years and then became president of the Youth Ushers. Now I'm in the Adult Ushers and I'm also president of the Young Adult Choir. I was in Youth Fellowship starting in 8th grade and I'm still in it in my junior year. [tape 5, p. 13]

As Kathryn's comments suggest, Grace Church's core experience for youth (and children) is the adult worship service on Sunday morning. This is the time during which a great many things happen, but chief among them, from the point of view of this book, is the opportunity for youth and children to see how their important adults openly prize their faith.

Because Grace Church's intent is to directly teach children about the rubrics of worship, the Bible, and the values of being "unashamedly Black and unapologetically Christian" (*Annual Report*, p. 19), Grace regularly brings children and youth into the adult Sunday service to lead that service. One way this is done is by encouraging participation in Little Warriors, the children's choir. They are told that they are an important part of the Sunday celebration. Their practice every Saturday is long and is marked by strong disciplinary commands from their director. Most of the songs are learned without sheet music. After observing three rehearsals, I reflected on my observations of the Little Warriors with an adult member from Grace Church:

> **Interviewer:** That choir director is tough on those kids. Today she said things like: "Don't you be talkin' with your neighbor, cause I know all the different tricks now. I can see you doing that, and if you talk to your neighbor during church, I'll stop the choir and ask you what you're doing." When the director asked, "Have I done that before?" everybody said, "Yeah."
>
> **Adult Member:** So it's serious; it's praising God and giving him the best we have.
>
> **Interviewer:** I hear you, but it came as a surprise to me to see the training. She tells the kids when to sway and when to clap. Maybe this is a racist comment, but if I, as a white, had walked in one Sunday when these kids were singing, without seeing this rehearsal, I'd have said, "That's spontaneous." But now when I've seen those little kids practicing I know that "spontaneity" has been developed out of a long history of Saturday afternoon work.
>
> **Adult Member:** Right. But it's more than that. I'm thinking about all that training we did with the kids at Grace on Saturdays, and it's hard work, but I'm also thinking that we do it Sunday after Sunday . . . I mean singing the Lord's Prayer and the Invocation; I mean the constant singing of responses in worship . . . so that it becomes *like a discipline.* The people at Grace encourage us . . . they say, "You're getting stronger!" But we're stronger because it's a part of who we are; we do it week after week. I hear you talk about the children rehearsing and working hard; and they really do rehearse, but they have to, because we want the choir to totally respond in worship.
>
> **Interviewer:** So that when the Little Warriors sing on a Sunday. . . .
>
> **Adult Member:** They help lead. Music is a very deep part of our people. [tape 1, p. 10]

It is clear that participants in the Little Warriors choir meet adults who believe that worship is important, and that children and youth help *lead* worship through their singing. Thus, children and youth are important contributors in worship. They work hard at their singing, so hard that adults reflect with them about worship not only as a celebrative response, but also as a responsive discipline.

It is also clear that adults and children do not regularly worship together—that is, children are not regularly visible in the "adult" Sunday worship service unless they are involved as part of a "youth Sunday." Youth Sunday occurs every fifth Sunday, in no particular order, so that (for example) while communion is being served "upstairs" in the "adults only" communion service, children from grades one through six are being instructed "downstairs" *in their own communion service, complete with the presence of an ordained pastor, in a parallel "Youth Church."* An *Annual Report* from 1984 notes:

> The purpose of the Youth Church Ministry is to provide a worship and learning experience for children during regular morning and afternoon services. Our objectives are to:
>
> a) Conduct a Black worship experience which will demonstrate and explain all of the elements and symbols of worship.
> b) Encourage Bible study and scripture memorization.
> c) Provide learn-and-do activities which reinforce the worship theme as well as illustrate the value of being unashamedly Black and unapologetically Christian.
>
> [1984 *Annual Report*, p. 19]

The intent of Youth Church seems clear. Youth Church is to be a worship experience within which trusted adults will instruct children about what it means to be black, to be Christian, and to be one who worships at Grace Church. Youth Church regularly occurs every Sunday during every adult service.

Observing Youth Church (which is for elementary children) on a Communion Sunday, I found thirty-seven children seated in ten rows of chairs facing a simple communion table. Music from the Little Warriors, the young adult, and the adult choirs, was being played on a tape recorder. Noting that communion was "serious business," an associate pastor named the specific elements that would occur in this worship service, asked if the children were "ready to begin," and then put on his robe while singing the opening song with the children.

The pastor quizzed the children regarding their memory verse (the same memory verse each month is shared with children and adults in worship); scripture was read, bread and juice were shared, prayer was offered, and the used glasses were collected. Throughout this sequence the pastor talked about the content of the service with the children. For example, when the offering was collected by the youthful ushers, the pastor gave everyone time to get money (and this meant, for some, the pastor helping them find money in snow pants; for others it meant finding coats or purses). After everyone had money, it was collected by two of the ushers. As the two ushers came forward, the minister said, "Would one of you be willing to pray over the money?" Neither child was willing to pray, so the pastor asked, "Do you want me to pray?" They said, "Yes," and he prayed.

After the pastor's prayer, volunteers were asked to step forward for a prayer circle. Half the children came forward and joined hands in a circle. Those who had not stepped forward were instructed to join hands with their neighbors. Since this was January, the pastor asked the children to pray for "something that God might help them with in the New Year." Starting the prayer, the pastor said, "I pray that God will help me be a better minister in the New Year." The child to his left in the circle prayed that she might "be a better student." The circle continued until everyone had an opportunity to state their prayers; a song was sung and the pastor asked the children to repeat, with him, the Benediction.

Following the Benediction everyone was asked to gather around several tables. Sweaters were sought by some children who were cold, while other children used this break to go to the bathroom. Punch and graham crackers were served. A short film about a boy who cheats on a test and who discovers that he does not feel good about such cheating was shown. In the film, the boy talks to his father and his teacher, and then feels better. The film was applauded.

Regathered around their tables, the children discussed "temptations" with their teachers in light of Ephesians 6:10-11 and "the armor of God." Sheets of paper, crayons, and Bibles were involved in the process of naming the content of such "armor." With the time that was left, the children colored their pictures, at which point they had been involved with Youth Church for over two hours. As the adult church communion service upstairs ended, choir members entered this room to take off their robes (because this is the room where the robes were stored). Other children also entered, arriving for the second Youth Church of the day. Because the first service was "running late," things trailed off into greetings from parents, goodbyes from teachers, and exchanges among children.

Asking an adult Grace Church member to share his understanding of Youth Church elicited the following response, written as if several children were presenting their understanding of Youth Church. Such an exercise indicates the values placed on Youth Church by Grace's adult members:

> We look forward to seeing and meeting each other every Sunday morning in Youth Church. This is different from Church School (which meets on Saturday mornings). Here

there are no grade divisions. We sit whereever there is a friend, and renew relationships from last week. Some of us are only six years old, while others of us are thirteen years old.

The church choir uses our space to hang up their coats and prepare themselves for the ministry of music, but when they leave for the early morning service upstairs, our altar is our own. This space becomes our Worship Center.

We gain a sense of control as our friends pass out Bibles to everyone, whether or not we have begun to read. Before the sermon starts, each one of us will have the correct page of the text for the day. Our parents do this upstairs in the Worship Center, and we are told their days of scriptural familiarity began early, like ours.

We volunteer for various activities. Some of us become readers of the scriptures. Some of us become collectors of the offering. One of us becomes the liturgist who opens the service. Others of us become monitors of the tape recorder which plays music prerecorded by us during one of the rehearsals of our own youth choir sessions. In other words, we listen to our own musical singing during the youth services. And then one of us gives the benediction at the conclusion of the service.

There are many things which appeal to us about these experiences. We do not have any parents to disturb us when we whisper to our neighbor. Our services are less than an hour, and then we have refreshments. This is followed by Bible quizzes or other projects which teach us a lot about the Bible. We have some real whizzes in our groups. We contend that we have a better knowledge of the characters in the Bible than do our parents. When we pray, God listens directly. There is a direct link from us to God. And even though some of us cannot read, it is meaningful and comforting to have the Bible in our hands while one of our friends reads to us.

The sermons are given by church ministers, and quite often by seminarians. They engage and involve us about the circumstances in which the scriptural text is set. And drawing upon our life experience, we verbalize and express

our impressions in comparison to what seems implied by
the text. We even see the similarities of the biblical times
to our own schools, homes, churches, and communities.

There are many special times during our services, but we
really enjoy taking time to be silent; during those times we
know that God comes into our midst. We really like it when
we volunteer to get into the prayer circle. This is the time
when our special prayers are heard by God while we are
holding hands and encircling the altar. We also pray before
and after taking up the offering. God blesses us with many
things, homes, schools, parents, teachers, and our church.
So, we understand and participate in contributing to pay
the expenses of the church, and we thank God for all of
[God's] blessings upon our lives.

We like the adult volunteers who assist in guiding us
through our youth services and the "after" programs.
When we grow up we are going to be just like them: i.e.,
patient, understanding, and helpful. They do not reject us
if we get playful. However, they do remind us where we are,
and that is fair.

Every fifth Sunday all of us go upstairs and are in charge of
the whole worship service. Our choirs provide the music
(the Little Warriors and the Young Adult Choir). My
friends, six and eight years old, are the liturgists; they open
the services, which are attended by our parents and other
adults of the church. One of our teenagers preaches the
sermon.

The adults of our church do these things for us knowing
that God loves us just as much as God loves them. Even
though we are very young, we know how, and want to pray
and sing to God also. We feel and know the presence of
Jesus in our lives. We know and are learning the differences
between truth and nontruth. Our church is a special place,
and we have a special place in our church. [document T]

In an interview, Pastor Able indicated that Youth Church
had "a pragmatic and an educational genesis. We outgrew
our building and didn't want to baby-sit our kids. We
wanted them to be in a meaningful setting and we also

needed seats for adults in the Sunday service, so one of our Christian educators designed an appropriate curriculum that was aware of our African-American context, and we linked this with a full-scale 'Youth Church' experience. So we have 'worship training' in Youth Church; a kind of 'boot camp' for our service. When the kids come 'upstairs' for a Sunday service, they know what is expected of them. They know how to behave in worship" (tape 6, p. 3).

Leading Worship

Grace Church emphasizes that when worship is recognized as a critical retelling of the faith community's story, then leading worship is a weighty responsibility. "When the children are told (and then experience) various forms of involvement in worship, then worship has been presented to them not only as a celebration, but also as a disciplined way to tell the story" (tape 6, p. 8). This is extended from childhood into adolescence as high school youth sing and preach at the Sunday service (high school youth volunteer to preach, roughly every fifth Sunday, in no set sequence). In effect, the variety of youth programs offered at Grace Church are built around participation in the adult Sunday morning worship experience. It is in the worship experience that the Christian tradition and story shapes and reshapes this community.

Opportunities to be a part of worship include the Young adult choir, interestingly composed of high school youth, but intentionally called "young *adult*" to emphasize the full role of these "young" *adults*, particularly in worship. Rehearsing once a week, these fifty youth have several youth directors, numerous soloists, elected officers, and a style that can only be described as high voltage. When I first observed a rehearsal, I was struck by the fact that while the music director and an associate pastor were present in the sanctuary, the youth themselves conducted their business

meeting, the prayer circles, the questions of who were or
were not members of the choir (and therefore eligible for
subsidy from the church for an upcoming weekend "retreat") as well as the direction of the rehearsal.
During the several times I visited rehearsal this pattern
held, with the associate pastor regularly giving the choir
short, open-ended teaching homilies. In my notes I summarized my observations in this fashion:

> The ordained pastor came to pray with the choir and to be
> the minister to the choir. But the young people held their
> business meeting by themselves; no other adult was present
> or told them what to do or not to do. They introduced
> things like, "We have to nominate somebody to be a
> chaplain," or "We have to get our officers straight and get
> ready for the year's work." And they had a discussion about
> who they ought to nominate, had nominations, and some
> discussion and concern about one person who was a
> representative (because she hadn't regularly been there),
> and what should they do about it? They had to figure out
> how to deal with her. And all that kind of stuff they did
> essentially by themselves. [field notes, p. 16]

It is but a short step from such regular responsibility to
the full responsibility of leading (and preaching) in a
Sunday morning service. A youth who recently read
scripture on a Sunday morning notes some of the parame-
ters connected with responsible worship leadership:

> After the service everybody was saying, "We're so glad we
> came. It was so wonderful and beautiful, you touched my
> heart and I just felt the Spirit spoke." And I said, "Well, I
> just gave a lesson." And so I thought, "I'm going to do this
> again. Let me do this one more time." And a lot of people
> started looking forward to hearing me again, and I'm glad
> that I decided to do that. The second time I spoke, a lot of
> people seemed to enjoy what I had to say. And then I
> actually preached, and everybody supported me in doing
> that. It's like when you grow up here.... It seems like I have
> five thousand parents, all watching me, because it seems
> like I know everybody. [tape 12, p. 2]

The power of such a regularized, intentional involvement of children (and then youth) within worship can be seen from the following description of a "fifth" Sunday, when youth were responsible for every phase of an adult-based "upstairs" morning worship, including the sermon.

Youth Sunday In the Sanctuary

Standing before the congregation, an enthusiastic elementary-aged boy loudly quotes, to much applause, the 137th Psalm. He is followed by a young girl, also elementary-aged, who calls the congregation to prayer. As the Lord's Prayer is given voice by this girl, the young adult choir responds antiphonally. Ending the Lord's Prayer with quiet statements of "Praise the Lord . . . Amen," the congregation holds its applause as a junior high girl begins to speak: "Blessed assurance. . . ." (from the congregation: "Yes, yes") . . . "Jesus is *mine* . . ." (soft applause) . . . "O, what a foretaste. . ." (more applause) . . . "of glory divine. . . ." Then the Little Warriors break into singing. One verse has been sung when the choir director, apparently not satisfied with the level of enthusiasm shown by the Little Warriors, stops their singing while stating: "I hear you saying, 'This is *my* story,' . . . and if you *believe* that it's *your* story, then you'll *sing* it!" Vigorously responding, the choir *sings*. As they reach the line, "all the day long," the director has them stretch out "long" to at least ten syllables.

One of the ordained ministers, robed and wearing denominational insignia, rises, greets the congregation, shares the monthly memory verse with them, points out a variety of announcements, and highlights the upcoming men's retreat. Guests are noted, and there is a "passing of the peace." As the young adult choir stands to sing, the minister sits down. When a young woman soloist sings "Touch me, Lord," the second verse is accompanied by soft clapping, with several congregants standing and swaying to the music. The choir sits, the music continues in the background, and new members come forward to join Grace Church. Sponsors stand beside each new member, and a communal statement is given voice by the congregation. Soft organ music continues, bracketing the "morning prayer" as offered by a high school student. She asks for God's "blessing," so that the young adult choir (which recently lost a member of that choir), can "understand" and "sing God's praises," even as they "put this member into the ground." As electronic organ music swells, members of the congregation softly respond, "Amen."

An Old Testament lesson is read, and the Little Warriors respond with "The King of Glory Shall Come in." Several solos are involved in the next young adult choir offering. These lines come through with great clarity:

> When the going gets rough,
> He's always there;
> That's why I love this man.
> Every day, with Jesus.

The collection is taken: youth ushers are in charge. After the reading from the New Testament, a high school youth offers a moment of rededication for those willing to "come to the altar." Many members of the congregation move into the aisles and come forward to the altar. Those who have not come forward are asked to "join hands with a neighbor and to offer, for them, a prayer of dedication." Waiting for a moment of silence, she quietly intones: "Hush, hush, Grace Church; somebody's calling your name." This is the opening line for a prayer that concludes with: "And be with my big brother as he brings your sermon this day . . . let the church say, Amen." And the church responds: "Amen!"

A final song before the sermon is offered by the Little Warriors. Again, applause and calls of "Amen" respond to this musical offering. A high school male stands to introduce the morning's preacher, Daryl Jenson. The student's comments about Daryl include the following observation: Daryl is a seventeen-year-old senior who attends a nearby public high school and who hopes to attend Arkansas University in the fall. With this "formal" introduction out of the way, the young man introducing Daryl offers a short, humorous story concerning Daryl, ending the introduction by saying, "And so, I give you 'Catfish' Jenson." Convulsed with friendly laughter, the congregation greets Daryl, "Catfish" Jenson, with applause.

Jenson begins: "Good morning, Grace Church." The congregation responds, "Good morning." Daryl offers his first line, "Black men are needed as role models in the church." There are scattered "Amens" and light applause. Pausing for a moment, Daryl Jenson makes his claim, "I speak on behalf of the Lord in all his goodness," and hesitates. "I *am* nervous," he confesses, to much applause and more laughter. Encouraged, he asks the congregation to "come together in a spirit of prayer," and prays for "God's support . . . to speak through me."

What unfolds through Daryl's sermon is a powerful testimony to Daryl's mother, Grace Church's programs for children and youth, the intentional ministry of the men of Grace Church, and the centrality of a sense of the sacred in Daryl's life. It was the programs and the activities, Daryl states, that kept him from "being an early parent, having to get married, tossed into jail, or into drugs." Noting how Grace Church "programs" (vacation Bible school, Saturday morning church school, the Little Warriors, scouting, building black men, the youth fellowship) paralleled his growth, Daryl emphasized that without programs like these, "growing up young and black in the big city would have been difficult." But, he confessed, "God and my mother are in conspiracy for my soul; she, in particular, blocked my ability to skip school, get into gangs, and do drugs."

The programs of Grace Church, Daryl's mother, and "the men of this church" spent a lot of time with Daryl. It was the men of the church who issued Daryl "an open invitation" to attend all the men's retreats. It was the men of the church who coached the Little League, went on the boy scout outings, and drove the church bus. The head usher, Homer Smith, had asked Daryl to "come help fry chicken." Daryl had agreed to help, but he had slept in on Sunday, so Homer checked with Daryl's mother, and Daryl was awakened and started frying chicken with the men of Grace Church. Daryl notes: "I helped cook and you asked me to all your meetings; I felt I was a member."

In a deft turnaround, Daryl states: "Now I will be going to college ... and *who will help cook chicken with the usher corps? Who will help in the men's fellowship?*" If this sounded like "empty rhetoric," Daryl is willing to offer "a covenant": "When I am home this next summer, I will drive the church van for Saturday church school; I will coach a Little League team; and I will help with the Little Warriors." Given this part of the covenant, Daryl asks: "Who will help Grace Church? Who, right now, will make a commitment? We need black men as role models in the church. Who will come forward?" And people sitting in the congregation rose up and came forward. Amid laughter, applause, organ music, and singing, Daryl was able to announce: "I've got four men and two women; that isn't enough. Who else will come forward?" And two more persons come forward.

As Daryl conversed with those who had come forward, one of the ordained pastors of the church took the microphone to say, "Let us thank God for using Daryl and leading him." Her prayer concluded, she states, "All of the men in the church should stand. Brothers! Note the young men who joined church this morning. Greet them following worship. They are to be guests on the men's retreat next Saturday. I hope you greet them in Jesus' name." As Daryl offers the benediction, there is continued music as all the choirs, the liturgists, and the ordained pastors recess to the front door, where they will greet the people.

The Pastor's Support

That children and youth regularly lead and preach in such worship experiences is in large part due to the support of the senior minister. Numerous persons indicated to me that many adults come to Grace to hear Pastor Able, and that when the church began involving high school youth as preachers every fifth Sunday, "people waltzed into church and were waiting for Pastor Able to speak, and when they saw all these kids marching in here, their faces dropped, and they weren't satisfied until Pastor Able kind of like played off the song, 'Oh Yes, We're So Glad We're Here,' and that kind of stuff" (tape 5, p. 10).

The pastor, in an interview, noted that when he first began involving youth in worship with responsibility for the morning sermon, he followed no regular preaching schedule, and persons would stop by the church to check the outdoor sign board "to see who was preaching" (tape 6, p. 11). "If they found out Bobby Jones was preaching instead of me," Pastor Able notes, "many would stay home" (tape 6, p. 11). When asked how he was able to change this negative response, Pastor Able says, "Through educating the church to their responsibility to youth, and—with a chuckle—by tearing down the signboard out front. Now no one knows who is preaching, and people come to worship God, not to hear a certain preacher" (tape 6, p. 11).

Pastor Able indicates that a youth's speaking on Sunday is a "tremendous educational and spiritual experience, not only for the youth, but for the church" (tape J, p. 4). He also indicates there is considerable risk involved, unless the church works with the youth: "The first time I asked the kids to choose someone to give the sermon, they chose someone outside our tradition who just happened to have attended one or two youth fellowship meetings. I was terrified at what I heard. The sermon was counter to most of what I believe. I said, 'This will not happen again.' So we set some guidelines. The kids: (a) must be active in church, active in youth fellowship, involved in stewardship, and passing their grades. Then (b) we assume a kid doesn't know how to preach unless we help them—so we hear the sermons in advance and give them pointers. We 'try it out' in the sanctuary. Now I can sit there without having a heart attack, because I know someone has worked with the speaker. We train them—and some of the most powerful messages in this church are preached by youth" (tape 6, pp. 5-6).

While not every youth will choose to preach or to be dramatically involved on youth Sunday, Grace Church's extension to them of this opportunity symbolically portrays children and youth as "having something to say" within the congregation. In addition, "calling a choir composed of high school students a 'young adult.choir' symbolically pulls youth into 'adult' worship" (conference tape, p. 16). On a regular basis this "young adult" choir leads worship; occasionally youth preach; on other Sundays, "They *are* in worship" (conference tape, p. 16).

CHAPTER
EIGHT

"IN" BUT NOT "OF" DOMINANT CULTURE

"Vision is the key element of our church's growth," says Pastor Able. Our 'Ten-Point Vision' suggests the church's energetic liveliness: A worshiping church, a spirit-filled church, a praying church, a tithing church, a Bible-based church, a progressive church, a politically aware church, a love-centered church, a stronger working church and a community and liberation conscious church."

Grace Church's Pastor Able,
*as quoted in the denominational
newsletter, November 1987, p. 5.*

On the surface, St. Andrew's and Grace Church have remarkable similarities—both are large, multistaff, professional, mainstream, middle-class, Protestant congregations. Both are surrounded by neat, well cared for homes, but if St. Andrew's and Grace Church were located in the same city, St. Andrew's would be two hundred streets and Grace Church one hundred streets from the center of that city. Thus, St. Andrew's is suburban, while Grace Church is urban. And one of the marks of urban professionals is that youth attend a variety of public and private high schools. Grace Church's youth are "scattered across this side of the city; some are in 'magnet' schools, while others attend Lutheran and Roman Catholic parochial schools. You name it, someone at Grace probably attends it" (tape 10, p. 3).

An adult sponsor of one of the youth programs fondly remembers the first time she was recognized outside Grace Church: "I was driving some distance from Grace on a Wednesday late afternoon, and I just happened to pull up at a red light, when the car beside me started honking. I looked over, and it was a carload of kids going to the young adult choir rehearsal at Grace. The driver rolled down her window and told me that she was picking up people from different schools. Four different schools were represented in that car; and they were having fun" (tape 10, p. 4). No single school dominates at Grace Church. In one sense, the wide mix of schools provides Grace an excellent opportunity to be uniquely open to everyone. Daryl, the speaker at the youth Sunday noted in the previous chapter, proudly mentions that "here, at Grace Church, is where my real friends are. These are the people I hang with . . . except for girl friends."

The mystique of the mall and the stress of the school are also felt by adolescents at Grace Church. Daryl's litany (early marriage, parenthood, drugs, or jail) adds, in this urban context, the message of the street. But Grace Church, while attended by some members of the "underclass" (a term not appreciated at Grace), can be described (fairly) as a professional, education-oriented middle-class church. Each year Grace presents dozens of scholarship/awards to those who are showing improvement or success in various educational settings. Many youth from Grace Church will go on to higher institutions of education, ranging from schools of business and nursing to four-year colleges and universities: "This is the educational expectation we have for the youth of this church; we know it will be hard, but we see this as a goal to be realized" (tape 8, p. 4).

Grace Church's Cultural Expectations

But the use of the word "middle-class" as an adequate descriptor of Grace Church is met with some anger by church members: "Most of us are only a paycheck from real problems," states one Grace Church adult (tape 10, p. 6). Money is not the real focus of concern regarding "middle-classness" at Grace Church. To seek "middle-classness" is, in the words of one Grace Church adult, "an attempt to join with those who rule . . . to become white . . . in a mindless pursuit of money" (tape 6, p. 4). This rationale implies that desperately seeking middle-classness can distance one from the nurturing roots that sustain a black's "real" identity. Indeed, Pastor Able understands the pursuit of middle-classness as having far-ranging cultural impact. For example, as Pastor Able describes how he was called to Grace (he is the second pastor in Grace's history), he stresses the one crucial factor presented to him by the lay committee: "They asked, Are we going to be a black church in a black community, or are we going to be a white church in a black community?" What they decided, said Pastor Able, "was to be a black church related to that community in every way. And they made a decision, literally handed me a job description saying—Can you do this and lead us in this direction in the black community?" (tape 8, p. 9).

This was a difficult task. Well aware that many blacks with middle-class aspirations were adopting at that time the dominant white Euro-centric worship expectations of his denomination, Pastor Able instead encouraged Grace to reconnect with its African heritage. Commenting on something that is a common experience at Grace today, but a radical experiment twenty-five years ago, Pastor Able remembered: "The first time that eight members said 'Amen' in church in the middle of the service (and not at the end of a prayer, but while somebody was preaching) all the heads turned to look" (tape 8, p. 8). While this provoked controversy and some immediate loss of membership, it also clarified the church's stance regarding "blackness." A Grace Church member notes: "Certain kinds of street language, saying Amen, and clapping, are looked on with chagrin by the white middle class and had been by those of

us aspiring to that status. Pastor Able tried to break that
kind of white expectation in this black church" (tape 3, p.
6).

Thus, twenty-five years ago, Grace Church consciously
embraced a black worshiping style, and intentionally became "a black church in a black community." Youth
ministry within this black church could never "be depart-
mentalized or split off from the central reason we are here,
and that means worshiping together, for it is in worship that
we discover spiritual sustenance in the midst of a culture
that offers no sustenance, even to the youth" (tape 8, p. 8).
The senior pastor puts it like this:

> We want persons coming into our midst to find us a source
> of spiritual sustenance, security, and inspiration and those
> participating in our spiritual-social process to be strength-
> ened in their commitment to serve as instruments of God
> and church in our communities and the world—confront-
> ing, transforming, and eliminating those things in our
> culture that lead to the dehumanization of persons. [docu-
> ment M, p. 3]

A Framework for Youth Ministry

From the beginning, Grace Church's youth ministry had
a dual grounding: (1) *worship*, with access to the pulpit every
fifth week; and (2) *political awareness*, with youth being
challenged to carry ministry "into" the world.

The emphasis on *worship* meant, among other things, a
consciously black (rather than white) "style" of worship.
Thus, children were trained to sing out of the oral tradition—without printed music and with appropriate motions
(tape 1, p. 10). Rhythm instruments and black gospel songs
were blended through worship "in the black style" (tape 3,
p. 6). "Youth Church" specifically emphasized biblical
literacy and adult worship practices at Grace Church.

As children entered adolescence, however, things
changed. Adolescent youth were reminded of their "pil-

grimage" when they joined a choir carefully demarcated as
the young *adult* choir. Here youth were treated very nearly
as peers by adults. Adult advisors advised but did not lead
this group. Leaders were the youth themselves who not
only assumed major responsibility for the choir, but who
also led worship in every way, including preaching Sunday's
sermon. Grace Church seemed to say that by the time
children reached adolescence they should be encouraged
to make major contributions within the church community. Such a process, Grace suggests, is the best way to have
an effective youth ministry.

In all of this, certain *boundaries* of the "black style" were
observed. For example, ecstatic movements and emotive
dancing (reminiscent of other "black traditions") were
perceived by Grace Church to be on the outer fringes of the
"black style" they sought to emulate, and were therefore
avoided. Still, within such clearly understood boundaries,
an intentional interpretation of the "black style" was embraced. For Grace Church, a pivotal understanding is that
"God can never, within this way of speaking about reality,
be controlled" (tape 1, p. 15). Worship at Grace Church,
while embracing a certain emotive "style," was never—in a
final sense—predictable or controllable.

This concentration on "spiritual sustenance" (document
M, p. 3), while clearly visible in worship and the groups and
activities that surround worship, is complemented in youth
ministry at Grace Church by (2) *the learning of political
prowess.* At Grace, youth are challenged to "serve as
instruments of God and church in our communities and
the world" (document M, p. 3). In addition to the regularized structures for social action within Grace Church, youth
are particularly involved in the political process within the
Youth Fellowship, other youth structures, and the denominational framework.

It is clear that the primary focus of Grace Church's youth
fellowship is political awareness: "We do go on retreats and

have fun, but a lot of what we do rotates around what's going on in the city, the world, and the church" (tape 6, p. 12). For example, youth who are involved at Grace attend United Black Christians (UBC), a denominational black caucus that meets monthly at denominational churches in the metropolitan area as well as annually at a nationally selected city. UBC used to be an adult-only caucus, but:

> In November of 1982, at the UBC Convention, it was voted that there would be a youth and young adult caucus because the youth felt the need to be noticed and to be listened to . . . because we have concerns ourselves that adults need to be aware of. So at the Convention it was voted that we have a youth and a young adult caucus at the national level. At the same time on the local levels there are now youth and youth adult caucuses. With our city chapter we have a youth and youth adult caucus. And we are very active in the planning of the convention coming up here in July." [tape 6, p. 13]

The monthly meetings are at different churches and serve as "youth rallies" with a political agenda. "Youth go to the meetings to keep very aware of what's going on. It's like business. You really get to say where and when and they discuss issues. And they vote on whether they should, like, take an issue of deep concern and help it out, or go to certain meetings, or things like that. It's the way we keep in touch with everything that's going on" (tape 6, pp. 8-9). This organization has made an impact locally and nationally. An *Annual Report* (1984) notes the political ability of the UBC:

> At the UBC Convention the youth were able to challenge leaders of different instrumentalities. The subject at hand was the Annual National Youth Event, sponsored by our denomination in July 29-August 2. Many of the black youth that participated in this event were concerned with the lack of ethnic diversity throughout the event. Our concern was ignored by the instrumentality heads. They were informed by letters, which most of them did not respond to until the

U.B.C. stood up on our behalf. We are very grateful for the United Black Christians and blessed to be a part of them. [tape 16, p. 2]

Thus, youth ministry at Grace seems to mean participating in worship through the choir while being politically active in the political processes of the youth fellowship, the UBC regional meetings, retreats, programs, and the ongoing social ministries of the church. Youth have leadership responsibilities in all these areas.

The Challenge of Grace Church

Grace summarizes its total ministry with the phrase: "unashamedly black and unapologetically Christian." To be "unashamedly black" is to understand one's history and to be politically aware. To be "unapologetically Christian" is to center one's life on God and to respond in worshipful ways. At a conference comparing St. Andrew's and Grace Church, attended by both black and white pastors, the black pastors noted that Grace's claim and its activities (black "style" worship, political involvement, open pulpit, and "fifth Sunday" youth leadership) were true of many black churches, but also noted that "the claims are not always so explicitly stated and interwoven throughout the fabric of the church" (conference tape, p. 14). In addition, these black pastors affirmed Grace's explicit assessment and implementation of "the black kinship heritage—of helping one another and telling the story in all of life's situations." They believed that the summing up statement of Grace Church ("unashamedly black, unapologetically Christian") was a clear challenge to the middle-class dominant culture— that is, "I am not ashamed of the gospel; I do not need to apologize for my blackness" (conference tape, p. 14).

The black pastors at that conference were significantly impressed by Grace Church's "open pulpit" for adolescents: "openness to the pulpit is *the* sign of how seriously

Grace is about youth ministry," said one pastor (conference tape, p. 15). One black pastor, a woman, stated: "This pastor's power is inherent in his clear articulation of a black style of ministry, but the bigger idea, the possibility of a shared ministry (an extended kinship network) involving everyone, is not only a key part of black history, but also follows the model of Christ. As Jesus taught his disciples and sent them out, so this black pastor *challenges* the members of Grace Church (who are, after all, middle-class) and sends them—both young and old—into ministry" (conference tape, p. 15).

People who come to Grace Church expect to be challenged by what happens there. Such expectations are born of experience, as I discovered when I observed the large Saturday morning church school program for children in grades one through six. As I met with the church school teachers prior to the children's arrival, I sat with them around a table in the church basement. When sixteen people were present, one person initiated what I later discovered to be a regular Grace Church devotional/ prayer ritual (named, from African tradition, an *UMOJA* circle). After reading a brief passage from the Bible, the leader bowed her head, grasped the hands of the persons sitting beside her, and began to pray for the success of that day's program, for one of the nonmember teachers who was present (that she might join the church), and for the continued presence of the Holy Spirit in the classroom. As she finished, the person to her left continued the prayer. When that person finished, the next person in the circle also prayed. By this time I had recognized that by clasping hands I had joined the prayer circle and had terminated my privileged "observer status." I was now a participant and was expected to join with the others in praying out loud. As the prayer "arrived" at my spot in the circle, I was in the position of having either to indicate in some fashion that the prayer circle should continue without my prayer, or that it would continue with my prayer. I chose to pray.

Whenever a prayer circle happens at Grace Church a complex interweaving of Christian tradition and African principles (in this case *UMOJA*, the African principle of unity) occurs. Such prayer circles are a common practice at Grace Church's meetings and programs. In notes made by me in the month of February I entered the following:

> Not only prior to Sunday worship, but prior to the young adult choir's rehearsal, there was a prayer circle. Prior to the Saturday church school program there also was a circle of prayer. There was a prayer circle at the board of Christian education's business meeting. One might think that these circles of prayer could become mundane after a while, and in fact, perhaps they do; but one of the things I am struck by is the reality of the kinds of prayers that are verbalized. What helped me "see" how confrontive and powerful this ritual act has become was when the young adult choir (the high school youth choir), without adult leadership, went through the same process; i.e., everyone joined together after a scripture verse, held hands and started praying. One new male choir member (introduced and welcomed earlier in the rehearsal), recognizing that he was being invited to hold hands with the male choir members on either side, raised his head and half stood up (as if to leave), but one member, already touching him, pulled him back into his chair. I think I know what he felt. [tape 13, p. 20]

At Grace the prayer circle regularly challenges those who dare to enter its sacred circle. There are expectations for those who grasp hands.

Sponsors

A "sponsor" reflects on how he was *challenged* by "the larger circle" of Grace Church:

> I became a Christian and a member of Grace in my teens in high school. And many of my friends were not and they would go towards the street action. But I found something

much better here that would keep me away from that. And
I'm very comfortable with it. This is, in a very real sense, my
family. And my "family" has put me in touch with the
world. I've attended local functions, regional and national.
In fact I'm now a member of the national council of this
denomination. I must say that it's been rewarding interact-
ing with these national leaders. . . . And here I am only
twenty-one years old. [tape 6, p. 9]

As a "graduate" of youth ministry at Grace Church, this
young man (who attends college near Grace) continues his
pilgrimage as a "sponsor" who is involved with the young
adult choir and the youth fellowship group. He is clear,
however, that his involvement with Grace Church goes
beyond youth ministry: "I attend the Bible study groups
with real seriousness. There are dozens of these groups,
and they are organized so that you can advance in your
understanding. And, of course, I am here every Sunday for
worship" (tape 6, p. 10). He is clear that "this is a form of
ministry I believe I have been called into" (tape 6, p. 10).
    While Grace Church hires no single ordained profes-
sional to "do" youth ministry, authorities (conference
ministers, seminary professors, professional youth ministers, members of Grace, and pastors at other churches)
agree that Grace has a powerful youth ministry. The key to
this phenomenon is the claim that *everyone* at Grace Church
is a minister, that ministry is an acknowledgment of the
divine in one's life, and that people are regularly "called" to
be involved in specific forms of ministry, one of which is a
caring ministry with youth. This "calling" may or may not
lead to ordained ministry; in the context of Grace Church,
it can lead to being a sponsor involved in a ministry with
youth. An adult sponsor, sharing her grandfather's teaching that "you must have a calling for ministry," quoted
Chapter 2 in Habakkuk regarding waiting for "the vision."
She noted that before she became a sponsor, she had been
asked, but knew that the Bible tells us to "wait; and even if
it is slow in coming, the vision will come. We always go to

God first" (tape 12, p. 4). When the "call" came, she responded.

Nearness and Directness

Stephen D. Jones, in *Faith Shaping: Nurturing the Faith Journey of Youth*, assumes that "ministry with youth means much more than working with the youth groups and classes. Perhaps most importantly, it involves coordinating and guiding a church's faith development emphasis."[1] By "faith development emphasis" Jones means, in part, a clarification and acceptance by the congregation of that community's "faith bias."[2] A "faith bias" is the particular faith stance of a specific congregation within a specific context. Jones would argue that not only by talking about faith but by living faith, believers bring faith *near* to youth. Jones puts it like this:

> There must be a nearness (closeness) to the faithful community and its traditions, rituals, and stories. *Being near to the faith is pivotal for youth.*
>
> The faith is near when Christian adults live their faith in natural ways before the young person. The faith is near when the young person feels that he or she is a close part of the church. The faith is near when the young person is allowed deep relationships with adult Christian models.... The faith is near when families are not embarrassed to express faith and when parents are public with their commitments. The faith is near when families develop and practice faithful traditions in the home with regularity. The faith is near when youth can see how much faith is prized by the important adults around them. The home and the church must be in harmony on the importance of faith.[3]

According to Jones, nearness (nurture) is only one part of what a congregational youth ministry model should expect from a congregation. A congregational ministry with youth will also be *direct* with youth:

Directness occurs when we intentionally aid young persons in writing a new chapter in their faith story. Directness means frank questions and discussions with youth about the meaning of personal faith. Directness includes occasions when worship is intimate, when prayer touches, when service is eye-opening. Directness happens when we intentionally (though it may be spontaneous) help youth address their own questions of faith. Directness occurs when we share our faith story and faith bias.[4]

A minister, reflecting on this process of "nearness and directness" as it unfolds at Grace Church, notes:

Grace is very clear about the purpose of youth ministry. When youth were kids they picked up important images of faith from their extended family of important adults. Grace is nurturing a kind of "kinship" idea of youth ministry. There is a kind of authority about those early connections with "aunts" and "uncles" that lasts until adolescence (when the child wants self-identity). Then the child/adult wants self-identity and needs to personally sort out whether the God and Jesus of their parents have the same meaning for them. . . . Now the kinship "circle" has built a powerful presence. In part, Grace's youth ministry is about this kinship circle helping youth in the process of figuring out how to do "imaging" of God, how to acquire God's true image and where to see that image in life's setting. [conference tape, p. 13]

Grace Church provides both "nearness" (the immersion in such interpretation), and "directness" (the challenge of specific words for particular occasions). Critical to this process are caring adult "sponsors" who have felt a "call" into this kind of "ministry." "Sponsors," in the words of one youth, are "those Christians who spend more time at church than they do anyplace else" (tape 6, p. 1). Adults who care in an extended family way volunteer to lead in the variety of Grace programs. To be a sponsor is to be seen as a person "who is right with the Lord and who is like a good 'uncle' or 'aunt'" (tape 7, p. 6). One youth notes: "The first sponsors I knew led Vacation Bible School in the summer.

I later found out that they took their two weeks of vacation to do this" (tape 7, p. 6). Another youth confirms the importance of the sponsor's role: "From the fifth-and sixth-grade leaders I learned that black was beautiful and that Africa was our motherland; when I was in Building Black Males I remember the shared experiences of the black men who sponsored us. Even these men of the church who weren't called 'sponsors' spent a lot of time with me" (tape 8, p. 1).

Grace Church is like a home away from home: "It seems like I have five thousand parents, all watching me, because it seems like I know everybody" (tape 12, p. 2). A young woman who has just reflected upon her involvement in a youth Sunday, exclaims: "It's pretty interesting when you grow up in a church; it's like your family expands. Like if I get locked out and leave my key in the house, I can come to church" (tape 4, p. 11).

Pastor Able, the senior minister at Grace Church, notes: "Today we have at Grace Church what we lovingly call alphabets, all alphabets—MDs, JDs, PhDs, ADCs. For us, we realize that those letters behind a person's name is how you make a living. As for us, the church is about *how you make a life*" (tape 12, p. 11). Pastor Able's message is rooted in the context (Pastor Able's words) of "the historical reality of who we are and where we came from" (tape 8, p. 11). Members of Grace Church hear this as the biblical call to be "in," but not "of," the dominant culture (tape 6, p. 8). Youth, seeing this, positively respond. One young adult, reflecting on Grace Church's leadership, comments: "Grace Church gives us the future, now. If you're told you're the future, but you just sit in a pew, then . . . who cares?" (tape 6, p. 14).

PART
THREE

BEING YOUNG, CHRISTIAN, AND AMERICAN

As "inheritors" of dominant culture, the members of St. Andrew's Anglo-American congregation offer youth a teaching agenda tacitly accepting the values of that culture.

Traditionally "outsiders" within dominant culture, the members of Grace Church's African-American congregation offer youth a teaching agenda explicitly challenging those same dominant cultural values.

By comparing and contrasting these dissimilar teaching agendas, chapter 9 provides a provocative curricular typology.

Suggesting that St. Andrew's accommodative stance toward dominant culture has weakened St. Andrew's to the point that it is unable to engage in public moral discourse, chapter 10 explores the value-laden issues of being young, Christian, and American within these two congregations.

CHAPTER
NINE

EXPLICIT AND IMPLICIT
TEACHING AGENDAS

Our human vocation is to be in partnership with God to fashion even as we are being fashioned, attempting to realize our artistic capacities as this happens. For to the question, "Who is fashioning?" the response is, "God and ourselves." And the medium we are asked to concentrate on here as the "stuff" or material of our work is the set of forms "traditioned" to us through the centuries by the Christian church, the set of forms that, taken together, comprise the curriculum of the church.

Maria Harris[1]

While both pastors have seminary degrees, Pastor Able of Grace Church continues his deep interest in musicology while Pastor Schmidt of St. Andrew's has a degree in business administration. These strengths, over time (the pastors have tenures of twenty-five and thirty years), have greatly impacted the nature of both congregations. But there also has been a "goodness-of-fit" with these senior pastors and their congregations: "We got what we wanted," indicates one Grace Church long-term member, "and we're happy with what happened" (tape 1, p. 12). "Pastor Schmidt built this church," reflects one Christian education committee member at St. Andrew's, "and he's done a good job" (tape 9, p. 7).

While understanding that other congregations may do things differently, neither St. Andrew's nor Grace Church envision major changes for the educational emphasis of their congregation. Indeed, Grace Church will continue to challenge people from the congregation's "unashamedly black and unapologetically Christian" stance. While there may be innovations and additions, youth ministry at Grace will remain critically reflective of the culture and intentionally direct in the centrality of its worship. Little is "hidden" in Grace Church's youth ministry: "We come right out with what we intend to do, and then we do it" (tape 1, p. 6). From these statements, we might infer that Grace Church has an *explicit* teaching agenda, and in this we would be correct.

On the other hand, St. Andrew's will continue to educate members of the congregation by managing its "cafeteria" approach of classes, programs, and workshops. In this respect, curriculum at St. Andrew's will avoid any clear or sharp reference to specific Christian or "religious" language. While there may be innovations and additions, youth ministry at St. Andrew's will continue to unreflectively embrace the culture while avoiding a regular involvement of youth in worship. Much remains "hidden" in St. Andrew's youth ministry: "We have no real curriculum; often we just sit around and have a good time" (tape 4, p. 3). From these reflections, we might infer that St. Andrew's has an *implicit* teaching agenda, and in this we would be correct.

Certainly both congregations are involved in giving implicit/ explicit messages, but while mounting an impressive array of youth programs, St. Andrew's is grounded in its tacit acceptance of "the way things are in our essentially good society" (tape 2, p. 4). Grace Church is dubious about this church/culture relationship, and is therefore more reflective, less tacit, and ultimately more intentional about "teaching."

Two Biblical Traditions

Charles R. Foster, writing about contemporary Christian educators and the thought of Walter Brueggemann, persuasively argues that people who experience stability and prosperity may celebrate God's graciousness and "the importance of responsibly managing the bounty of God's goodness" out of one of two specific traditions that are deeply anchored in the Old Testament experience.[2] Foster puts it like this:

> In an era of social, political, and economic stability and when the blessings of life seemed abundant, Hebrew expectations of educators were [that they might] celebrate the "gifts already given," and to seek for ways to preserve them for the future. From this perspective, educators were not as concerned with the urgency of rehearsing and interpreting the national heritage for a new situation. Instead they emphasized the *management of environments for learning* that people might discover ways to maintain and extend the blessings of life.[3]

Foster's conclusion is that frequently Christian educators, in times of prosperity, instead of engaging in the uncertainties offered by problem-posing education, are called upon by churches to "manage" informative programs within that church's tacit embrace of the dominant culture. St. Andrew's, with an MBA (master of business administration) at the helm, relies upon a "cafeteria" approach to education, an apt metaphor for those experiencing the abundant blessings of life.

But a second biblical tradition, noted by Foster in the same article, suggests a provocative framework for those who teach within "a strange land." This second tradition argues for critical, intentional teaching:

> [With the tribe or nation] at the brink of extinction the educator remembered and rehearsed for the people those stories that reclaimed and affirmed their corporate iden-

tity, meaning, and purpose. The educator interpreted
those ancient stories for the critical situation in which the
people now found themselves and instructed the people in
what they must know and do if once again they might
escape the bondage or oppression they now experienced.
In a sense, the educator acted to preserve the corporate
memory and to conserve the corporate identity, not to
perpetuate the past, but *to alter the current situation and
experience of people.*[4]

Such intentional teaching occurs at Grace Church, where
youth are deliberately involved in worship at an early age.
Sharing the black cultural history, lifting up the "kinship"
story of a people who helped one another while challenging
the status quo, Grace Church and its pastor (with his deep
interest and ability in musicology) "sing and pray and act—
remembering who we are—through these hard times" (tape
1, p. 8).

Thus, while similarities and contrasts abound, both
models of youth ministry are related in specific but different ways to the dominant American culture. The white
"corporation" model of youth ministry (utilizing a professional youth minister) unreflectively strives to transmit a
culture that, by and large, has blessed the members of St.
Andrew's. The black "extended kinship" model of youth
ministry at Grace Church (dependent in large part upon
cross-generational "fictive kin") critically distances itself
from a culture that has proven, again and again, to be
untrustworthy.

The white model's *implicit* (and culturally blessed agenda)
teaches five dispositions that support the unreflective trans-
mittal of that culture; the black model's *explicit* (and necessary for cultural survival) agenda teaches five dispositions
that equip "African-American Christians."

Grace Church's Explicit Teaching Agenda

1. *The Importance of Being Unashamedly Black*

Being "unashamedly black" is interpreted and reinforced at Grace Church by the use of a long list of "African Principles" and "Black Values." These are to be taught and emulated as part of the "reeducation process" through which Grace's members might "peel off some of the middle-class virtues and be reeducated to African principles and black values within the Christian church" (tape 1, p. 6). For example, "Each month in Youth Church we deal with African principles. In teaching the word 'faith' we teach it as the African word *Imani*" (tape 3, p. 12). And *Imani*, notes a Grace adult, is "something other than white middle-classness. So we name such black values to our children in the hope they won't venture into white middle-classness" (tape 3, p. 25). Another adult notes what happens when a black attempts to join white middle-classness: "Oh ... then they're just kinda stuck in limbo, out of the family, and when you're not accepted in the class or white culture that you thought you were going to get into. ... So you're just out there; but the door is always open for that person to come back (tape 1, pp. 17-18).

Grace Church's Pastor Able consistently focuses upon "the historical reality of who we are and where we came from" (tape 8, p. 11). And the congregation is asked to pass this message on to their children by modeling black Christian behavior: "Preaching the word means being involved [says Pastor Able] in a constant struggle against my people being dominated" (tape 3, p. 12). Every month, memory verses from the Bible are shared; biblical language is continuously quoted and used in all Grace Church pamphlets and reports; every sermon is "biblically centered and filled with the language of the faith community" (tape 3, p. 12). There is no apology for this: "much of what we do is community identification ... we all know it. We preach on it. We refer to it" (tape 3, p. 6). And the "it" of this quote is the shared common faith language and black experience (the story) of the Grace Church community.

At Grace, music often serves as "the starting point for the story" (conference tape, p. 14). Grace's music connects within African tradition and the gospel story. Celebration within this fusion "includes the whole body—voice, movement, storytelling, history, and heritage. The idea is to pass on the heritage through many different means while focusing on the story" (conference tape, p. 15).

Singing several lines from the song "Ain't Nobody's Fault But Mine," one Grace Church adult noted that: "faith is passed on in song; the message is carried in the story" (tape 12, p. 13). She reviewed how the black church rehearses for worship. She recounted her own experience as a young person hearing the pentecostal service and practicing what she saw: "My friends and I felt that something was happening; we might not have known what, but something was happening and it was important to practice what went on in order to get it right" (tape 12, p. 15). Telling me that religious language and symbols have no meaning if the people have not heard the "informing story," she concluded with these words: "music is a critical way through which the black church has always emphasized the story" (tape 12, p. 15).

2. The Importance of Being Unapologetically Christian

People arriving at Grace Church are challenged by its "religious" thrust. For example, I had my "observer status" challenged when I chose to become part of the Sunday school teacher's "*UMOJA* Circle." In that instance the challenge of the church was clear: whenever a prayer circle occurs at Grace Church, a complex interweaving of Christian tradition and African principles (in this case *UMOJA*, the African principle of unity) takes place, through which certain expectations are explicitly presented: anyone who grasps the hands of those in such a circle comes to understand that they are joining with an intentional unashamedly black body of believers who view prayer as a powerful connection between God and their church body, who expect that concerns presented by the body will receive responses from God, and who normatively pray out loud.

By providing a variety of ritual containers (like the *UMOJA* prayer circle, as well as ORITA ceremonies[5]), and a variety of programatic frameworks (like Saturday church school and Sunday youth church), Grace Church designs a path through which children and youth can be "immersed" and come to know the language, customs, and history of Grace Church's faith community. The rituals are explained to children and youth by both lay and ordained ritual leaders. Every time a prayer circle occurs it is suggested that this is how "we"—that is, everyone here, this is how "we"— pray. At the same time, programatic frameworks lift up the "important things" that are to be known by every member of the community: memory content from the Bible, stories of the African-American experience, and the celebration of worship.

Being "spiritually alive" has the highest priority at Grace Church. This means, for example, that "young adults" (the high school youth) are completely responsible for the Sunday adult worship service every month in which there are five Sundays. The senior pastor picks the date; it could be "the fourth or the fifth or the first, but he picks it and it's never announced ahead of time" (tape 5, p. 10). On that Sunday youth are responsible for everything, including the sermon. "Juniors and sophomores have given some sermons. One of the ministers or advisors just asks, like, is there anyone who wants to give the sermon on such and such a date. Most people are kind of backing away or at least thinking seriously about it" (tape 6, p. 6). Another youth notes: "I'll read the scripture, because I don't know if I'm ready . . . at least *that* ready" (tape 8, p. 11).

The adults of Grace Church recognize that "it is rare to have such openness in worship" (tape 1, p. 16): "Black congregations often have authoritarian male ministers . . . and that's the only person allowed to preach. At Grace Church the minister is different; his mind is much broader than that. By his openness he models a different way of being. He has the larger vision" (tape 1, p. 15). No one questions the senior minister's authority or power within Grace (in fact, Grace is often referred to as "his" church); but this senior minister chooses to weave his authority within the congregational "kinship" fabric as a shared task. In this, the pastor is very progressive.

Pastors considering such a move ask hard questions: "For the black church, finances are important. Many are struggling to keep the church open and the preaching is vital to having people give money to support the church. An adolescent preacher may negatively affect the amount of money given and this could be serious for many black churches" (conference tape, p. 17). Comments like this one suggest how important and symbolic an open pulpit at Grace can be for black youth.

3. The Importance of Being a Competent Leader

While there are issues yet to be resolved at Grace Church (for some, Grace has not been radical "enough" in its response to its community—that is, Grace's political rhetoric sometimes seems more profound than its activity), Grace Church's understanding of the role of youth ministry within the congregation resists mainstream insularity and safety in favor of promoting more adultlike ministry responsibilities for youth. At Grace, faith is a lively and shared participatory event giving youth important and prized roles to play within the faith community. A variety of opportunities for high school youth exist in connection with Grace Church's Sunday morning worship experience. These include the young adult choir (composed of high school youth, but intentionally called "young *adult*" to emphasize the full role of these "young" *adults*, particularly in worship). The youth themselves have critical roles in the running of the choir. They run the meeting and direct the rehearsals. A youth advisor confirmed my observation with these words: "Many churches mouth the words 'train up a child in the way he should go,' but then expect youth to get it by osmosis. Grace Church's intent is to empower youth now so that we have permanent leaders in the years to come" (tape 6, p. 13).

Youth understand, but sometimes have mixed emotions. One youth put it like this: "I know the responsibility is good for me. Look at all the things I'm doing! It will help me get into school and everything, knowing that you can have those very important roles in this church. I guess that's pretty good and will help me when I get ready for college; I mean, to know that I can do certain things without anybody's help" (tape 5, p. 3).

Whenever a new program, event, or issue occurs at Grace Church, youth are included. When I observed adults initiating a "chaplaincy" system for each adult Grace Church program, I was aware that youth were to be involved in running that same system in all the youth programs at Grace. Several weeks after its inception, I observed the following discussion at the young adult choir:

> During the young adult choir's business meeting, one young woman raised the issue of "needing a chaplain." Several persons questioned "what that meant." She explained, noting that "each program, including ours," would have a chaplain, "to pay attention to the group's spiritual life and to lift up issues as they happen to the larger church community." Discussion was ended by the nomination of "a new chaplain"; after the vote, the group seemed to say to the chaplain, "We'll support you; we aren't exactly sure what you'll do, but we'll support you." [field notes, p. 16]

An officer from the young adult choir suggested that the adults of Grace Church:

> know what they are doing, because they're kind of like telling us that you can take an office in a youth organization at the church and you have to be totally in charge, and you also have to learn to work with each other. And not rely so much on adult input but your input, and try to compromise with what you have. They treat us like we're young adults, and I like that. [tape 5, p. 4]

In this process, youth within Grace's worshiping community are treated more like adult members and less like children. This is primarily because the adults believe faith is intimately interconnected with life, and that "faith is carried through experiences, words, and traditions, and that *youth must be able to 'do it.'* In authentically black models of youth ministry like Grace Church, the young people are expected *to do* the ministry; some failures will occur, but they must try it" (conference tape, p. 13). Such a "nurturing, facilitating, and enabling ministry enables youth to publicly own their faith" (conference tape, p. 14).

4. The Importance of Being Politically Aware

Every fourth Sunday the youth fellowship meets following the adult worship service. Unlike agendas for most youth fellowships, this is the business meeting of the youth at Grace Church; "This is the time when we come together to plan our agenda" (tape 6, p. 4). Worship services, denominational activities, occasional social events, political rallies, summer camps, and the like, all get planned at this meeting. As such it becomes the pragmatic point from which youth organize their activities. In addition, here is where youth work the political process at Grace, in their denomination and at the national level.

Grace Church opens youth to a wider understanding of their world. This occurs in a variety of ways, ranging from the "Free South Africa" sign on a front lawn to the Sunday bulletin, which serves as a community newspaper. It is not uncommon for that bulletin to run from ten to twenty pages, and be filled with articles ranging from "where to get volunteer income tax assistance" to "Apartheid's War." Political comments are expected from the pulpit and at Grace a "Church in Society Committee" can make the following political statement:

> The committee believes that the church, Grace Church in particular, must be a voice in the community, in society, advocating Jesus Christ. If you share our deep and abiding Imani [faith] and if you are committed to love and justice among his children—join us, the Committee for Church in Society. If you are committed to African people wherever they are found—committed to Third World liberation—committed to equality here in this country, in this city, committed to the principles of Malcolm and Martin, add your voice of *Imani* to ours, the Committee for Church in Society—with *Imani* and through *Imani* we can make it happen. [1984 *Annual Report*, p. 59]

While the primary goal of Grace Church is worship instead of social activism, involving youth in the political process "is in keeping with the black heritage of Moses and Sojourner Truth, and is present at Grace Church" (conference tape, p. 17). Therefore, "youth are asked to participate and lead in various advocacy programs while developing a role for themselves in the process" (conference tape, p. 18). One black pastor, however, wondered "how deep such transformation" went. He stated: "Grace isn't a radical church. It's main thrust is 'our' worship" (conference tape, p. 16).

Another black pastor continued this criticism by observing: "This particular church is trying to 'save' black folks. This may have social implications for the larger society, but that larger society is not their main goal. There are black groups trying to buy property and stores in an intentional effort to change the cultural setting, but not this church" (conference tape, p. 18). Others argued that while Grace is not a "radical" presence in the larger community, it actively supports various social ministries and currently is involved in building senior citizens' housing, so it is not surprising that members "believe that Christ is the liberator and that they are called to go forth and transform others. They hold the hope of changing the world—they work for ending apartheid and for having a world where all can live together as God's beloved" (tape 1, p. 20).

5. The Importance of Making a Life

While Grace Church does have numerous political advocacy groups in place, they believe the "most profound political act of this church is the rejection of the white, non-spiritual, middle-class striving for personal success" (tape 1, p. 20). They feel the radical nature of "retelling the Christian story without being assimilated into the larger culture is the single most important focus of the church's role in youth ministry" (tape 1, p. 20). An intentional black ministry at Grace Church articulates the struggle of the black middle class in its effort to remember the African-American Christian story.

Grace, through the preachments of its senior minister, Pastor Able, regularly notes the dangers of attempted assimilation. In his sermons he names "black middle-income-ness" as acceptable while showing how those who strive to become white and middle class will fail. For Pastor Able, an effective black youth ministry involves the continual effort of wrestling meaning from a life marked by the reality of slavery and prejudice.

Grace Church's *Church School Handbook* (1984/85) notes that historically the black church is one of the "most vital Black institutions in the United States and the one place

Black people could be fully men and women" (p. 9). The black church offered, in the *Handbook's* words:

> Not only spiritual sustenance but also various societies, educational experiences for young and old, charity to the less fortunate, church school, suppers, plays, concerts, and so forth. Men and women could be slaves or shine shoes six days a week, but when they came to their church on Sunday as Deacon Jones or Elder Harris they were important and special people. It is this interdependency of the church and the personal and social life of the individual that is so African in character. [*Church School Handbook*, p. 9]

Grace Church emphasizes the church as "a place where people *count*" (tape 2, p. 6). There are many roles available for those who seek involvement, and many of these are named as "ministries of the church." The biblical story is critical for wrestling meaning from such a context: "People are seen as pilgrims on a lifelong faith journey, and the need to tell the story is still dominant in most black churches. When a person visits a black church they ask, "Can he say it?" "Can he tell the story?" They are looking for something they can hold on to" (conference tape, p. 14). Grace Church is a place where people come to hear "the story that informs our lives" (tape 1, p. 6). "Grace Church is a place to gather survival tools, meet people, and center your life. All of this amounts to passing on the tradition. Something is happening in that setting that is different from what happens in the outside world. The medium may be the same (story/ music), but there is something special about the local black church. That specialness is that Grace Church is supposed to deliver the story" (conference tape, p. 14).

St. Andrew's Implicit Teaching Agenda

1. The Importance of Being Middle-Class

"Crest is Best," Crestwood High School's kerygmatic motto, signifies that it considers itself to be a "top" school, capable of doing anything it sets out to do. Ninety-six percent of St. Andrew's youth attend Crestwood High School. Stepping into the Crestwood High School entry-way, a visitor is immediately surrounded by walls lined with competitive academic scores, athletic trophies, and clean-cut polite young men and women. In all this, Crest *is* best, and by so being properly communicates the values of the surrounding Crestwood community. A high school junior puts it like this:

> Pressure comes from a lot of parents because they want you to succeed. They say, "You have such a better opportunity than me and just look what I did; I brought myself up! . . ."

> So, if you want to have a good job and if you want to make it in the world, you're gonna have to get good grades so you can go to a good school so you can get a good job, so you can support yourself well and live in the same lifestyle that you're used to which, I think, is gonna be harder and harder to do. . . . Because it was so much easier for our parents, even though they had to struggle. But now that we're already here [living in Crestwood], where can we go from here? It seems like a cycle that's never gonna stop to me. . . . I mean, after you get out of college you're in competition to get a good job. And after you get that job you're in competition to go higher and higher and higher and get more money and more responsibility and more power, and it's tiring just to think about it. But I don't know what people can do about that; I mean, that's the way parents are around here. That's the way they started out, you know. [tape 5, pp. 80-81]

Crest's principal, Dr. Cardinal, suggests that since education has been a key factor for many of Crestwood's up-wardly mobile parents, it now becomes the focus of an inordinate amount of parental pressure for their own children to either hold their own or move ahead. He suggests that problems like mononucleosis, depression, stress, drugs, and suicide are obvious companion symptoms of such pressure (tape 15A, p. 4). For Dr. Cardinal, the school is a direct reflection of the culture that surrounds it. This, for him, is a mixed blessing—he sits in the middle of a place where education is highly valued and yet he sits (in the same place) where youth are ripped apart because of expectations to succeed.

The same high school junior quoted above would agree with Dr. Cardinal. She states: "I don't know how people handle it, I really don't. If they go home and they cry into their pillow every night . . . or just what they do. I guess if they're like me they just keep pluggin' along. . . . It'll end soon, but it won't" (tape 5, p. 9). During our year of research, the junior (above, tape 5) dropped out of a church youth program at St. Andrew's because both she and her mother knew she needed a better school record to get into college.

2. *The Importance of Being Morally Good*

That "one must be a morally responsible person" is a theme permeating the Senior High Fellowship. The base of this understanding is a sensing of "the religious" as a horizontal fellowship—that is, while there is little reference by adults within the church to the vertical or transcendent aspects of religion, there is much stock put in the human "celebration" centered in the coming and remaining together of the group. This is a "good" place to be, states one member of the group. "I am accepted here; we are like a family" (tape 13, p. 4). "No one would intentionally hurt anyone here," says another youth, "we care too much for one another" (tape 4, p. 6).

This sense of morality within "our" community was tested when two ninth-graders on their first senior high "lock-in" (an overnighter held at St. Andrew's) brought alcohol and cigarettes in violation of church policy. When the advisors discovered this via the offenders' parents at a later date, one advisor met with the offenders and "told them basically that such behavior is dumb and that I was surprised. They looked like I'd shot their dog when I started talking to them about this. I only took about ten minutes to do it and it worked to the point that if this thing occurred again it would be taken out of Jack's and my hands and go to the governing board. They responded very well" (tape 3, p. 7). The advisors assumed the story was common knowledge in the church, but viewed the incident as a good learning moment: "You can't dwell on those things. Somebody screwed up—every 15-year-old in the world screws up and we try and point out the fact that now we're going on; and in fact after that ten minutes we had about an hour of the best planning session we'd ever had" (tape 3, p. 8).

In retrospect, a curious statement was made by one youth regarding this incident: "I know there are some people in the youth group who probably drink. I know there are, but they don't do it at church. I'm so angry, and I thought, 'You stupid idiots, if you really needed to drink that much, why don't you just go to somebody's house and *have a party like normal people*, or whatever?' They just took advantage of the situation" (tape 3, p. 10).

3. The Importance of Being a Competent Manager

While applauding Crest High School's polite, hardworking, responsible "good kid" image, and operating the church as a "social place," St. Andrew's recognizes that life is a pyramid in which one either succeeds or fails. To negotiate the pyramid one needs managerial skills; St. Andrew's therefore provides youth with a place for management training.

There are few, if any, overtly "religious" words on our tapes. People from St. Andrew's note this absence and comment:

> We do have a lack of any faith talk, unless it's in a structured way—like in worship or in the Kerygma class. The lack of such language does have a ring to what our meetings are like. Kind of "here's what we need to do, let's do it!" language. I don't know that there are many people that aren't comfortable with that. Whether that's right or wrong, I don't know. I guess they get it other ways. Their expectations are fulfilled; I think *most of the people around here are verbal enough to let us know if they don't like it.* [tape 20, p. 9]

And that's just the point—everyone who stays is comfortable with the managerial, professional language. When there is a problem, St. Andrew's mobilizes its resources and responds with managerial savvy. Meetings have a "here's what we need to do, let's do it" tone (tape 16, p. 9). "We mount the resources and the staff, and solve the problem. We manage well" (tape 16, p. 7). St. Andrew's adults "pass on" managerial skills with youth serving as, for want of a better term, junior executives.

In similar fashion, while the youth committee used to be all adults (which the current chairperson thinks was "kind of funny" [tape 1, p. 14]), today's youth committee is composed of a small group of involved adults and a like number of youth. The chairperson does not want a big committee. She prefers to go to individuals outside the committee for specific requests. Thus, a small committee composed equally of youth and adults keeps "the young people from being overshadowed by a lot of adults" (tape 1, pp. 13-14) and is managerially oriented:

> The committee is made up of adults and young people and we really are looking at programs for youth, looking at some different things that they would like to do. For example, we have a church basketball league that uses our gymnasium. The young people decided that a potential way to make money would be to have a concession stand at the basketball games. And they're thinking of using the monies for their work trip which they take in the summer (tape 10, p. 1).

The youth committee focuses on developing and doing programs. When we asked why youth came to St. Andrew's, the kids often referred to this high level of activity—the work camps, the basketball leagues, bake sales, ski trips, the family clothes tree, the bell choirs, and so forth. One advisor put it like this: "We're always busy doing something and it always seems like when you're putting things together or organizing, nothing is going to work. But I have never come up against a situation when the actual time comes and it doesn't work just fine" (tape 3, p. 10). In effect, St. Andrew's teaches that one must be a competent manager to "succeed" within the cultural system. Youth learn how to "do it well" by being involved with committees and program processes at St. Andrew's. The adults understand this, saying:

> It's something that I have been pushing and when you study the committees of the church, I ask the committee to tell the youth what they do for them and to think about what the youth can do for them. And I ask the question . . . "Do you?" . . . each time someone comes in, "Do you pick a commissioned young person to be on your committee?" And they say, "Oh yes, start them young." I believe you can do this if you want to." [tape 19, p. 8]

4. The Importance of Being Friendly

When asked about the youth ministry program at St. Andrew's, Jack, the youth minister, responds that "youth ministry here includes fifth-graders through high school aged youth" (tape 19, p. 6). Jack further states, "I am responsible for all programs starting with St. Andrew's Saints, the fifth- and sixth-grade programs designed to mix kids from many different grade schools into one positive activity at St. Andrew's" (tape 19, p. 6). One parent organizer summarizes the "Saints" program: "Here children from the fifth and sixth grades meet on a quarterly basis for hayrides, hot dog roasts, bike rides, or whatever. The goal is to provide a social opportunity for the kids to get to know each other and play, you know; just play and have a good time" (tape 1, p. 8). Forty to fifty kids come together for such social activities.

The parents, in particular, support this program. "They are most excited about it, and say, 'Oh, let me know whatever I can do'" (tape 1, p. 8). By involving the children in such social activities, the St. Andrew's Saints committee believes the children's social relationships can be strengthened and that "perhaps the children will later continue on in their Christian faith by participating in the youth chorus, fellowships, and other social activities" (*Annual Report*, 1983, p. 15). St. Andrew's clearly transmits to youth the high priority of such "social" activity. The fourth-, fifth-, and sixth-grade St. Andrew's Saints program is well received by the parents. The up-front marketing technique employed is that "church is a fun place to attend; here is where you can make some friends."

Continuing the "social-mixer" format, the Junior High Fellowship steers clear of "religious" material, unless the youth pastor "sneaks" it in. The advisors are clear on this point—they are not comfortable with any religious language and prefer the social atmosphere. Providing a safe space away from Southtown Mall, the teen center continues to accent church primarily as a social place. Here youth can have everything Southtown Mall offers, including food, physical activity, video games, movies, friends, and excitement, plus loud music and a place to dance, all the while under the approving eye of parents. In addition, the Junior High Youth Fellowship relies upon church as a place to sell doughnuts and recycle paper, not as an aid to worship or as an ecologically sound project, but as a means to raise money for their annual social "theme park" trip. The St. Andrew's

1983 *Annual Church Report* summed up the totality of the Junior High Fellowship with these words:

> 1983 proved to be a good year for the Junior High Fellowship. A great big thank you goes to our advisors. Without their help we would not have had the quality of programing we did. . . . The junior highs ventured to "Worlds of Fun" in Kansas City on their spring trip. Many of the participants went free or at a reduced cost because of their outstanding fund-raising activities. The Junior High Fellowship continues to sell donuts on Sunday mornings. And their paper drives in the spring and fall proved to be very successful. [*Annual Report*, 1983, p. 16]

The importance of "being social" continues every Sunday evening as the senior highs come together in their Senior High Fellowship. Four advisors run the program "with a very good group of about fifteen to twenty regular attendees" (tape 3, p. 2). This year saw a big influx of ninth-graders from the junior high program. One advisor reflects on how the year is going: "The group changed, both in composition and in average age, so we spent a lot of time getting people to play volleyball or sit around and talk. We try and have a social activity every Sunday. We had a cookout and we're at the place where we held a lock-in a couple of weeks ago that they really enjoyed" (tape 3, p. 3).

5. *The Importance of Not Being Different*

Jack, the youth minister, points out that the predominant cultural system is "not just the school. There's no bad guy here; you've got the parents; you've got the school; you've got the kids themselves; you've even got the church in some respect; and they are all a mirror of the particular kind of upward climbing cultural pressure to succeed, be educated, do it well" (tape 15A, p. 14). Jack believes that what is at stake is a cultural vision of what it means to succeed in

America. The adults who are members at St. Andrew's are the people who have pursued the vision and presumably won; they will pass on the vision to their children. Their children are to become unreflective, cultural inheritors.

Perhaps Jack, the youth minister, focuses the issue most sharply. In one interview (tape 15A, p. 18), Jack shared what for him was a watershed event. He had set up a process for critically reflecting upon the culture in one of his first confirmation/commissioning retreats. The process entailed having a loop of rope tied upon one wrist of every retreat participant so that everyone was "bound" together. After a short hike, taken while bound, the group sat upon the floor, reflecting on what bound each person. Some were bound by personal issues ("I'm too fat," "I have problems with my family"). Others were bound by cultural concerns ("I'm afraid of war," "I don't think I'll ever marry"). Still others mentioned global issues ("This world is scary," "I'm afraid of acid rain"). But after a lengthy discussion over cultural symbols, Jack cut each rope while saying these words, "Whatever binds you, Christ frees you." When this experience was shared after the retreat by the youth in their homes with their parents, the response was largely negative.

In effect, Jack was later told that such experience was inappropriate. As Jack spoke (in retrospect) about this event and the parents' response, he articulated it as a rejection of his priestly, intentionally religious role. With irony Jack noted that events like this led him to believe that his role at the church was to be that of primarily an administrator of innocuous programs. No one, in his opinion, wanted any part of "transformation." In his words, "no one here wants to change" (tape 15A, p. 25).

A Comparison of the Two Agendas

In summary, the "teaching agenda" for St. Andrew's (implicitly taught), and the "teaching agenda" for Grace Church (explicitly taught) can be compared and contrasted in the following manner:

St. Andrew's
(white context)

implicit teaching agenda:

A. Being Middle-Class. The real world is competitively shaped like a pyramid with high school a microcosm of the necessary climb to the top; the church dislikes but accepts this form as reality. Many church programs structurally mime/mirror the pyramid form of the dominant culture. Success in the pyramid is honored.

B. Being Morally Good. There are normative moral codes (one does not drink alcohol at church youth programs for such activity threatens the "job" of the professional youth minister); church helps youth untangle the complexity of such codes; obedience is emphasized.

Grace Church
(black context)

explicit teaching agenda:

A. Being Unashamedly Black. Those blacks who seek to become white by joining the climb into middle-classness will exist in limbo. The church intentionally counters this issue by teaching black values and African principles; among them: the centrality of the helping tradition and the "kin"/"extended family" system.

B. Being Unapologetically Christian. There is no sacred/secular split; the church directly challenges youth to ground their existence within the Christian story; Bible study and worship are to accompany ministry as a "calling"; the church is one's "home away from home."

St. Andrew's *(continued)*

C. Being a Competent Manager. The managerial "know-how" of the corporation is the best way to be successful; the church structures and affirms opportunities for youth to acquire the skills associated with this metaphor: youth are expected to serve on committees, raise money, and do well in school.

D. Being Friendly. Church is always "social"—that is, a fun place to be. There are many adult-directed social activities at church. A professional is hired to "direct the youth program"; this person must be warm and caring.

E. Not Being Different. Adults blessed by the culture expect youth to inherit the blessing; church ceremonially rehearses their cultural story without encouraging the possibility of transformation (personally or systemically). The focus of adolescence is getting through it without "coming untracked." To be "tracked" is to go to college.

Grace Church *(continued)*

C. Being a Competent Adult. Leading worship, one's own group, and fully participating in all the "adult" programs of the church is the best way to move into a fuller understanding of Christian adulthood; the church intentionally provides frameworks that emphasize treating youth more like adults and less like children.

D. Being Politically Aware. To survive (in the dominant culture) youth must critically reflect upon the political process; the church forms youth into political awareness groups within the church and denomination. Youth fellowship provides youth with a political base in the church.

E. Making a Life. Historically the black church was an extended family where (despite the dominant culture) persons could be somebody; the church provides youth immersion in that relational intimacy; every youth intentionally carries Grace Church's message: "We are unashamedly Black and unapologetically Christian" into the world.

These "teaching agendas" highlight normative understandings of the "shoulds" and "oughts" of two churches'
realities. The youth of St. Andrew's and Grace Church,
engaged in an interpretive process, negotiate these agendas
as they move, more or less successfully, through adolescence.

CHAPTER
TEN

YOUTH MINISTRY IN AMERICA

The bravest kind of people I know are people who will ask those very difficult questions of themselves. We're not trained to do that in our culture. We're trained to have all the answers. We like the questions simple, like "Where's the mall?"

Sam Phillips[1]

In his book *Treasure in Earthen Vessels,* James Gustafson suggests that when a community intentionally conveys the meaning of the words, symbols, stories, and actions that are key to its existence, then the ongoing life of that community occurs not only through its outward allegiance to these signs and symbols, but also through "an inner continuity of persons through the ages who have understood and relived the same events."[2] How such a process occurs has been of great concern to youth ministers and religious educators, and has often resulted in efforts by them to provide a "best" methodology for shaping and controlling the dynamics of this interpretive process.

Early on, Anglo Americans had a clear vision of the correct methodology to use as the church intentionally sought to convey the meaning of God's kingdom upon this earth.[3] In search of what Martin E. Marty has called "the Righteous Empire,"[4] these persons attempted to *break* the individual's will to fit the kingdom. This thrust demanded evidence of an early *conversion* experience—even in children. Charles R. Foster has noted how this effort to break the individual's will required methods of education that centered on suppression. Therefore, suggests Foster, "the exercise of law became the necessary prelude to the experience of grace."[5]

While some ministers still continued to emphasize conversion in the shaping of the will to fit the kingdom, by the middle of the 1800s a second possibility, that of Bushnell's idea of *nurture*, emerged as a preferred means. Bushnell expected the home and church to "so surround children with proper influences that they would grow up to be Christians . . . without ever knowing themselves to be otherwise."[6] Instead of *breaking* the will, one could *bend* it. By the early 1900s, many who followed Bushnell's nurture approach were also favorably impressed with how well the emerging public school system professionally controlled the shaping of those who were now called *adolescents*.

A third approach emerged as nurture began to be identified with the professional educator's emphasis on *growth*; this approach would not "break" or merely "nurture," one would adopt the best contemporary tools to influence religious growth and development. Learning "experiences" were designed to evoke and reinforce the inherent goodness of participants. As Foster indicates, however, "this third view has been especially popular among professional religious educators who have been influenced by the insights from personality and learning theories, depth psychology, and the more optimistic views of human nature in the more liberal theologies."[7]

The end result of this third approach (the controlling of growth) has yet to be realized. In its wake, with growing recognition and admiration of professional educators, came the founding of the Religious Education Association in 1903. Mainline congregations built model classrooms, bought age-appropriate progressive curricula, supported the professionalization of Christian educators, and provided the necessary organizational frameworks for adult-controlled, developmentally sound, nationally designed, and locally managed youth fellowships.

This early twentieth-century Anglo-American movement emphasized a subtle shift in understanding the place of nurture—that is, the responsibility for nurturing adolescent Christians had moved from the broad societal context of home, community, and church to a more professionally maintained and adult-controlled church school and youth fellowship. Following this design meant avoiding the implications of the church as a community of faith—where a common, cross-generational "language" was spoken in an ongoing process of communal interpretation. Nevertheless, numerous congregations accepted and ultimately lost their voices following this scenario, in part because of their yearning to have control like the professional Anglo-American educators, and in part from the resulting age-graded isolation of children and youth from the ongoing life experience of the faith community.[8]

As did many other Anglo, middle-class, mainstream congregations, churches like St. Andrew's wholeheartedly embraced this third (professionally controlled, developmental growth) methodology. With this occurrence, these churches often surrendered their more organic shape (as "family," "body," or as "broken bread") to the emergent schooling, therapeutic, and marketing metaphors employed by the controller of age-graded growth par excellence, the public high school. Without fully understanding the potential problems associated with such overidentification with the public school, churches like St. Andrew's found themselves having professional educators and ordained ministers who administered the problems of producing and maintaining ever-increasing numbers of programs for growing children and adolescents while noting—with some distress—how seldom distinctive religious words, metaphors, or stories occurred within such programs.[9]

African-American Style

Ella Mitchell, in her provocative article "Oral Tradition: Legacy of Faith for the Black Church," notes how easily black Sunday church schools mistakenly patterned themselves after such white "schooling" middle-class models in the postslavery years:

> Black Sunday Schools were altogether too dependent on the externals of early white Sunday Schools as a model. These reflected none of the unique styles and needs of blacks. Rather, they emphasized gimmicks and whoopla such as competition for attendance and offering banners. These were the pride and joy of a middle-class religiosity committed to a culture of fierce competition in business and industry. It bore little resemblance to the extended-family mentality of African-Americans, but they bought it hook, line, and sinker. In their eagerness to give their young the best, they forgot that "white is not always right" either educationally or spiritually.[10]

Contrasting her experience against this white style of "educating" by telling about the two grandmothers of her early childhood home, Mitchell notes how they, without "benefit of printed curriculum or trained church school teachers," carried "the truths of the gospel in their very bones."[11]

In contemplating the "teaching methodology" that impacted these two grandmothers, Mitchell emphasizes the importance of cultural heritage, suggesting that only by "looking from within today's African traditional culture, one can discern with accuracy the broad outline of *world view and teaching* method which were brought to these shores two and three centuries ago."[12] Observing contemporary Ibadan children, Mitchell underscores the contemporary importance of African storytelling, audience participation, poetry, music, dancing, and drumming, while noting that interaction permeates every form. As Mitchell compared her Ibadan experience with Western-style performance, she was struck by the pervasive sense of "great enjoyment and expression of feeling. . . . They were surrounded by the lesson, and this was so natural they didn't recognize it as instruction."[13] "Being *surrounded* by the lesson" carried into the blend of West African roots and the necessities of the American slavery experience. The extended family "kin" system and the slave quarters with its closely shared living space paralleled, in intensity, "the intimacy of the small African family/village."[14] Yet, Mitchell adds, within this "group" setting, every child came to also understand the *importance of oral self-expression*: "slaves learned the value of expressing themselves just to affirm their personal being and power to act. . . . It was a way of clinging to a spark of vibrancy in a life otherwise often unpleasant."[15]

Today, African-American congregations interested in the implications of such a "teaching methodology," grounded in black "style," must remember how an earlier black culture assumed the importance of oral knowledge and interwove the spoken word (storytelling, proverbs, poetry, history, and preaching) within music and lively call-and-response, all the while encouraging interaction among the people present (as if all were part of one large extended intergenerational "kin" family).

Some implications could be drawn from such a black educative "style" if one were to design a black model for youth ministry aware of such a rich heritage. For example, the grounding assumptions for any such ministry would include: (1) the transforming and transcendent power of the gospel within an often hostile culture, (2) the possibility of youth speaking from the pulpit in a worship celebration engaged in intense, emotive verbal communication, (3) purposeful singing, and (4) the intimate presence of an extended, nurturing congregational family, (5) in which every adult becomes "kin," adults who are mutually responsive in faith with every youth or child. Grace Church, within its particular context, assumes many of these grounding assumptions as its own.

The Anglo-American Dilemma

In 1941 H. Shelton Smith wrote *Faith and Nurture*, a book that suggested the then powerful religious education movement would collapse unless educators recognized that "religious liberalism" had "lost much of its vitality in *training children for the good life*."[16] With roots deep into the eighteenth century, "religious liberalism" was understood by Smith to emphasize: (1) the *immanence* of God (God is intimately involved in the world) over the *transcendence* of God (God is wholly other, high and lifted up), (2) the *certainty of progressive growth* resulting in the coming of the kingdom of God (an individual, social, and cultural "moral age"), (3) the *goodness of humanity* (instead of humanity's sinfulness), and (4) the pursuit for the *historical Jesus*.[17]

While once a powerful theological and national force, the dilution of religious liberalism through two world wars, neoorthodoxy, and the uncertainties of the contemporary era resulted in a less coherent and more fragmented picture, even though many mainstream, Anglo churches in this country continue to operate as if the liberal understanding of reality is still the country's dominant vision. Unfortunately, an unreflective acceptance of the liberal vision by churches like St. Andrew's has had dire consequences for ministry with white youth. First, while the *immanence* of God necessarily accentuates God's presence in the midst of life, a church like St. Andrew's often unreflectively assumes that theological language can be equated with managerial language—that is, St. Andrew's has no theological distance from which it can critically reflect on God's presence in the midst of life.

Second, while the use of *growth* to visualize the ushering in of God's kingdom is a helpful metaphor, St. Andrew's (and other churches) tends to equate American middle-class existence with membership in that kingdom. When this occurs, "growth" no longer is a metaphor, and "democratic nurture and Christian nurture . . . became but two different names for essentially the same thing."[18] At this point, nurturing St. Andrew's adolescents into competitive, American middle-class citizenship unfortunately is understood to be the same as nurturing adolescents into the Christian faith.

Third, while the *goodness* of humanity needed to be emphasized as a counterbalance for those groups who were responding to the eighteenth- and nineteenth-century understanding of conversion, an overidentification with personal and social goodness can result in a kind of "we-are-good" enclave mentality (our class is good; our race is good; our church is good; our God is good).

Fourth, while the rational pursuit of the *historical Jesus* opened the church to the rigors of biblical criticism, religious educators tended to produce images of Jesus as the "master teacher," a kind of benevolent "Mr. Chips" who had a one-sided view of child development that suggested that the "little children" were already in possession of the kingdom of God.[19]

In all four categories, liberals, like St. Andrew's, trust in the rationality and rightness of the educative process. Education is taken seriously, and "at the heart of this faith in education is the assumption that the problems of collective existence can largely be solved by techniques of social fellowship and group discussion."[20]

What Language Informs the Church?

In *Habits of the Heart*, Robert N. Bellah suggests that the once ascendant "language" of citizenship and religious values in this nation is no longer ascendant.[21] In its place is the "language" associated with what he calls the autonomous middle-class American embrace of corporate and therapeutic individualism. Using extensive interviews with white, middle-class Americans, Bellah and his associates contrast this "first language" (born of hard-nosed, bottom-line corporate utilitarianism and self-oriented therapeutic individualism) with a "second language" (a biblical/civic republican mixture with its notion of the self being more fully realized in and through community, public forms of service, and commitment with and to other people). To the extent that this "second language" of communal and civic responsibility is weakened or largely absent from the contemporary scene, Bellah and his associates seek a renewed emphasis on citizenship and religious values.

In *Habits* Bellah documents some of the same issues raised by this book. He points out, for example, that between the Civil War and World War I, nothing less than a new national society came into being. During this time America was transformed from an agrarian society into a national marketplace. We expanded that market through accepting the claims of "Manifest Destiny" as a viable foreign policy. In the words of Isabel Rogers: "So we decided: take over the Philippines. And we did. Take over Cuba. Nicaragua. This was all seen as our special responsibility on God's behalf, and so our imperialistic tendencies became identified with God's will. Sheer idolatry."[22]

While *Habits* only deals peripherally with blacks, this time frame (from the end of the Civil War until World War I) was critical in defining what role freed blacks might have in this country. The rise of a managerial class and its dominant ethos—an individualistic climbing of the "ladders" associated with corporate America in pursuit of "success"—was deeply rooted in a technical post-Civil War progressive expansion, a prosperity not shared by blacks. In fact, regarding blacks from post-Civil War Reconstruction up to World War I, James P. Comer notes:

> Much of the land and potential wealth of America was given away while blacks were either in slavery or recovering from

the effects of slavery. Almost all of it was dispensed before 1915, when 90 per cent of the black population lived in extreme poverty and oppression in the Deep South. White people acquired the primary wealth in America, and the powerful few who got it were able to determine who would procure the secondary wealth; who would receive education and training; who would be employed; in short, who would be able to take care of their families.[23]

In the midst of this ferment, the corporation came to dominate the business world and "the self-made man of means became the legitimizing symbol for some of the aspiring middle class."[24] Blacks were guaranteed seats on the bottom of the economic ladder, not because of what they as individuals had done or had not done, but because they were members of a group that was now systematically subordinated by social structures.

While Bellah and his associates trace that part of the "first language" of corporate utilitarianism to such social/historical roots, they do not want to jettison that language, even if the metaphors employed frequently result in destructive behavior. Bellah's hope is that people might become "multilingual"—that is, he understands "utilitarian" and "expressive" individualism as useful in certain areas. He notes: "they only become destructive when they become general languages of moral and political discussion and crowd out considerations better expressed by biblical religion and civic republicanism."[25]

James Gustafson is equally emphatic regarding the importance of language. A church, Gustafson claims, "does not exist in any random gathering of people with a common ethos. The community is identifiable as the Church because *particular* meanings inform the personal lives of members and their life together."[26] Gustafson continues: if a church "equates the meanings of its language too easily with that of another community it risks the loss of its identity."[27] For Gustafson, "the Church's social identity depends, then, upon a twofold process: the continued use of the Biblical language within the common life of the Church, and its use in interpreting and understanding general human experience as it exists outside the Church."[28]

On Being Christian and American

It is at this point that St. Andrew's and Grace Church diverge: Grace Church intentionally accentuates its critique of the culture, while St. Andrew's embraces a culture in which it claims entitlement. The consequence of such a position for St. Andrew's, in Gustafson's language, is that it has chosen to avoid the consequences of *moral discourse*. In *moral* discourse "we are concerned with the direction of human activity in the light of an understanding of what is right and wrong, what is better and worse."[29] Gustafson is clear: "the language of command and obedience, of responsibility, of good and evil, of right and wrong, better and worse, are part of this language of morals."[30] For Gustafson, a church needs to be involved in moral discourse in order to help its members "discern between the more and the less worthy centers of loyalty, the more and the less worthy secular perspectives on politics and economic life; the more and the less trustworthy cultural values.[31]

At this point, however, St. Andrew's will not follow Gustafson's advice, primarily because its tacit assumption is that the differences between it and the culture to which it belongs are marginal, at best. Indeed, we have seen (chapter 4) that forerunners of St. Andrew's, persons like Horace Mann and Horace Bushnell, came to view education as an American missionary endeavor in the propagation of white, liberal Christian culture, and as a pragmatic means for rubbing off the rough edges of Roman Catholic immigrants and others (like blacks).

Some African Americans, however, continue to resist this effort at homogenization. For example, in *Black Children: Their Roots, Culture, and Learning Styles*, Janice E. Hale-Benson argues that African Americans participate in a cultural black "style" that has its distinctive roots in West Africa, "gives rise to distinctive modes of child-rearing among African-American people," and implies that bridges ought to be built "between the natural learning styles in the family and the novel styles of learning introduced in the schools."[32] Suggesting that an "analytic-cognitive" style is the approach to learning preferred by Anglo schools, Hale-Benson emphasizes, "not only does the school reward the development of the analytic style of processing information, but its overall ideology and environment reinforces behaviors associated with that style."[33] Assuming that there are other styles that "work" in formal educational settings, among them the more verbal, relational, and expressive styles of the African-American community, Hale-Benson is clear: she advocates the same high standards for black and white students, but she believes persons "cut out of a different cloth" ought to be met by the school with educational forms open to their unique learning style.[34]

Such a "black style" position has never been taken seriously by dominant American culture. Assuming that a common educational experience would favorably control (shape by *bending*) what it meant to be a Christian and an American, Mann initiated, and Bushnell (along with many others) supported a common school in which *no dichotomy would exist between being Christian and being American.* Charles R. Foster suggests that while we publicly adhere to a rigid separation of church and state, "the interdependence of religion and the public persists to this day. For many it functions as a moral force building up the national life in what Bushnell once called *the principle of loyalty.*"[35] Perhaps Bushnell's "principle of loyalty" resurfaces at St. Andrew's in contemporary guise as cultural and religious ethnocentrism—that is, there is no difference in the expectation of Crestwood High School and St. Andrew's Church. This means, of course, that St. Andrew's does not need or want to be about the business of providing, in Gustafson's words, a "theological language of interpretation" with which to critique the culture. In essence, St. Andrew's seems to say, "We *are* the dominant culture and we are satisfied."

In an article critical of this position, Dorothy Bass suggests that while some may view this interpenetration of church and culture as laudable, even praiseworthy, others, however (and here read Bass, Gustafson, Bellah, Foster, and this author), sense the *unreflective acceptance* of the words, metaphors, patterns, and the abandonment of any "moral discourse" at this juncture to be frightening aspects of the present situation.[36]

In particular, blacks wonder at how a "congregation" can so easily accept the loss of tension between the church and its culture. The African American Amos Jones Jr. notes how he has "often wondered how the contemporary Anglo church could promote the placement of the American flag and the Christian flag side by side in the sanctuary of a Christian church." "My understanding," Jones continues, "of the New Testament church is that such would never have happened."[37] Jones muses: "In effect, this was to say in the religious teaching of the Anglo church that there was [is] no dichotomy between being Christian and being American." And he makes an interesting leap into his history as he remembers that it was the early white missionaries among the slaves who insisted that "there was nothing inconsistent with being a slave and Christian at the same time."[38]

Two Congregations In America

Both Grace Church and St. Andrew's are alike in that they have retained strong senior pastors for fifteen or more years, have sizable (1,500-4,500 member) congregations, and are middle-class churches in predominantly white mainline denominations (United Church of Christ and Presbyterian Church U.S.A.). Both congregations consider themselves to be "progressive" and to offer what could be called a liberal alternative to their more conservative neighbors.

Grace Church, however, is more conscious of the impact of culture and its "social issues." It promotes critical reflection upon its own "middle-classness" and the roles a powerful black congregation in an urban setting might play within its essentially white denomination. St. Andrew's, on the other hand, accepts and confirms its favored position within culture, offering youth an unreflective enculturation process that encourages them to responsibly manage that which has been given. St. Andrew's implicitly hones this managerial role, chiefly through its understanding of "program" as "ministry." Grace Church disagrees with this stance and articulates its role with youth as a "ministry" in which the senior minister is expected to know the black "style" of religious education and therefore to be the chief ritual elder in the congregation's spiritual embrace of youth. Worship is the enculturating "kinship" core of this ministry, a place where youth are expected to be present, and are encouraged, through a multilevel approach including the possibility of them preaching, to become involved in "telling the story." At Grace, as at St. Andrew's, a youth is "immersed" in the process. The process, however, is not the same for both churches.

St. Andrew's "white styled" youth ministry relies on a hired youth professional to direct its youth program. Its model takes the form of a pyramid. Such a form emphasizes the importance of the hired professional (usually male, but not always), who resides at the top of the pyramid.[39] We have seen how the youth pastor at St. Andrew's, offering youth a vision contrary to the one employed by the church's senior pastor, found a stressful situation and the work load connected with this model overwhelming. This was accentuated by his countercultural conception of youth minister as pastor and ritual leader, an image shattered by the senior pastor's belief that ministry consists of administrative management. St. Andrew's avoidance of the youth minister's language of spiritual transformation suggested that his was the contrary vision, and he resigned.

Before resigning, the youth minister at St. Andrew's gently nudged that congregation toward more "ministerial and religious" involvement in youth ministry through his "peer ministry staffs." In that such staffs did not have a clear and critical view of the potentially transformative role they might play in the lives of youth, such staffs tended to fall back on what they already "knew"—that is, the content of their process, in that context—and remained predisposed to the values of the dominant culture, the white "style," and the figurative model of the corporation. I would hunch that a more radical model—for example, forming a mixed community of adults and youth in an ongoing exploration (by both the youth *and the adults*) of the transformative role of faith within St. Andrew's context—would have moved Jack Jeffries into open conflict with his senior pastor. Only such a move—over time—has the possibility of offering an alternative to youth ministry as a series of carefully managed and controlling programs, a "corporation," reproducing the cultural messages. This could take the form of something as simple, yet as complex, as "Bible study." Such a radical move could also encourage that variety of authentic intergenerational stances through which a youth comes to recognize faith.

The Implications of "Style"

While there are many models of youth ministry available to churches, each model contains deep assumptions about race, class, culture, the language of faith, and how it is or is not present.[40] While a church's blind or uncritical adoption of a particular model could miss the issue of cultural "style" within their unique context, churches rarely are consciously aware of the value-laden implications of style. In part, this is because churches like St. Andrew's, growing within a *favorable* cultural setting, accept the style of the dominant Anglo culture to which St. Andrew's "belongs." Thus members of churches like St. Andrew's, comfortable within their uncritical yet dominant cultural positions, are predisposed toward something like a figurative "corporation" model of youth ministry, a model that mirrors certain aspects of the dominant cultural white middle-class agenda.

If this can be stated about Anglo-American St. Andrew's and churches like it, what can be said about churches like African-American Grace Church? Following Paulo Freire, such churches (located within unfavorable cultural contexts) might "identify with the oppressor"—that is, such churches might adopt models like the corporation model in order to become more "like" the dominant culture.[41] In fact, there are many African-American churches that use Anglo middle-class models of youth ministry for precisely this reason. "It is possible," agreed one conference participant, "to have black churches looking like the white model." She continued, "If parents are unreflectively upwardly mobile, they will want to pattern their church on such a white model, unless someone provides them with a critical alternative" (conference tape, p. 13). Another conference participant noted that "more African-American churches use the Grace Church model than do Anglo churches; but that doesn't mean much, because there are certainly some Black churches that can be seen using the St. Andrew's white corporation model. But then, they are usually striving for middle-class status" (conference tape, p. 18).

In another context, I have stated: "While it follows that a model built with 'white style' normally cannot be transplanted into a consciously black youth context, there are black congregations which attempt to use white style models of youth ministry. Critics of such congregations claim those who adopt white styles of youth ministry are tacitly accommodating the white culture's value system. In any case, a white style model is not value neutral. Unless it is radically redirected, it carries values antagonistic to the implications of black style."[42]

Because every adult in the Grace Church congregation is seen to be a critical part of youth ministry, and because the faithful congregation remains at the center of this "black-styled" model, this form of congregational youth ministry can be visualized as a "family" or "kinship" model. Highly relational and affiliative in style, such a model confronts every adult believer with the congregational responsibility for "telling the story" with youth in appropriately near and direct ways. The congregation functions as a collective "parent and minister to youth." No single minister or team of adults "does" youth ministry. This important responsibility belongs to the entire church. *Everyone* is an "aunt" or "uncle," a youth minister, a spiritual elder.

From an Anglo point of view, this model is theologically attractive but programatically and pragmatically messy. Who picks up the pieces when particular families and specific youth fall through the congregational cracks? In many respects, the "kinship" youth ministry model is a small church model demanding faithful relationships engaged in active role-modeling intimacy and, as such, assumes that it can care, in faith-shaping ways, for its youth. This assumption may be the model's weakness. Few congregations actually embody such a vision, and those that do usually are led by very powerful ministers. Grace Church has just such a powerful charismatic leader. Pastor Able passes the tasks of administration to a competent associate pastor (who is a woman) and concentrates on how the spiritual pilgrimage of Grace Church might continue into uncharted areas.

Powerful ministers and so-called faithful congregations, like Grace Church, with a known "faith bias," often assume countercultural positions. Such positions often provide important reasons for bringing faith *near* and *direct* to youth.[43] The specific content of such models might fit within H. Richard Niebuhr's concepts of Christ "against, in paradox, or in transformation" of culture.[44] Grace Church would be comfortable within these descriptive characteristics. Sometimes, in its argument with middle-classness and radicalism, Grace Church skirts what Roozen, McKinney, and Carroll call an "activist" position in an effort to blend together "civic" and "sanctuary" positions—that is, Grace is not a radical congregation, and while it espouses "transformation," it does so within a "good citizen" orientation while remaining firmly anchored in the centrality of worship.[45] "Here," Grace Church states, "is where you make a life" (tape 12, p. 11). Thus, while this form of youth ministry sometime avoids the cultural entrapment of other models, it leads, via its "faith bias" and its powerful minister, toward a different set of issues. Without noting specific content, the hidden assumptions of the "kinship" model encourage the possibility of critical reflection upon cultural contexts as well as transformations via God and God's people. One can expect Grace Church to challenge people through what Charles Foster has called the transformative process of "altering the current situation and experience of people."[46] Such a model, therefore, might result in highly idiosyncratic, countercultural cultic expressions that could be considered healthy or dangerous, depending on one's point of view.

That Grace Church is *not* a bizarre countercultural expression validates the model as something that "mainline" denominational churches should not hastily dismiss. The above reflection, however, makes clear that such a model cannot be viewed as just "another program" or as something that "might work if only led by a professional minister." Instead, the cumulative weight of this model presses toward a church deeply grounded by its social-historical "style" and caught up in its faithful response to

God. "Good news" is determined, in large part, by context. In the words of my colleague, Susan Brooks Thistlethwaite, "the boundaries of difference need to be respected." The *avoidance* by Anglo congregations, however, of the variety of styles and models of youth ministry available to today's congregation suggests something other than respect. Until Anglo congregations (like St. Andrew's) recognize that their embrace of dominant cultural values is an excuse to avoid the implications of racism in America, youth ministry will unfortunately remain nothing more than a church-sponsored process of cultural transmission. We should expect more from the church.

NOTES

Preface

1. Dorene Doerre Ross, "An Introduction to Curriculum Criticism," in *Qualitative Research in Education: Focus and Methods*, eds. Robert R. Sherman and Rodman B. Webb (New York: Falmer Press, 1988), pp. 165-66.
2. Dean Hoge, "Five Differences Between Black and White Protestant Youth." *Affirmation*, ed. Sara P. Little, Union Theological Seminary in Virginia, vol. 2, no. 1 (Spring 1989), p. 80.
3. Ibid., pp. 82-83.

Introduction

1. David Elkind, *All Grown Up and No Place to Go: Teenagers in Crisis* (Reading, Mass: Addison-Wesley, 1984); Arthur G. Powell, Eleanor Farrar, and David K. Cohen, *The Shopping Mall High School: Winners and Losers in the Educational Marketplace* (Boston: Houghton Mifflin Co., 1985).
2. Robert N. Bellah, Richard Madsen, William M. Sullivan, Ann Swidler, and Steven M. Tipton, *Habits of the Heart: Individualism and Commitment in American Life* (Berkeley: University of California Press, 1985), pp. 62-65; Wade Clark Roof and William McKinney, *American Mainline Religion: Its Changing Shape and Future* (New Brunswick: Rutgers University Press, 1987), pp. 46-47, 55-56, 61-63.
3. *We Have This Ministry: A View Toward Youth in the Church's Ministry* (New York: National Council of the Churches of Christ in the United States of America, 1964), pp. 13, 16-18.
4. Ibid., p. 13.
5. Charles R. Foster and Grant S. Shockley, *Working with Black Youth: Opportunities for Ministry* (Nashville: Abingdon Press, 1989); Jeffrey D. Jones, *Youth Ministry: Making and Shaping Disciples* (Valley Forge: Judson Press, 1986); William Myers, *Theological Themes of Youth Ministry* (New York: Pilgrim Press, 1987); David Ng, *Youth in the Community of Disciples* (Valley Forge: Judson Press, 1984); Charles M. Shelton, *Adolescent Spirituality: Pastoral Ministry for High School and College Youth* (Chicago: Loyola University Press, 1983); Michael Warren, *Youth, Gospel, Liberation* (New York: Harper & Row, 1987).

Prologue

1. Richard Osmer, "Challenges to Youth Ministry in the Mainline Churches: Thought Provokers." *Affirmation*, ed. Sara P. Little, Union Theological Seminary in Virginia, vol. 2, no. 1 (Spring 1989), p. 5.
2. Martin E. Marty, "Reformed America and America Reformed." *The Reformed Journal*, vol. 39, issue 3 (March 1989), p.9.
3. Ibid.
4. Joseph F. Kett, *Rites of Passage: Adolescence in America, 1790 to the Present* (New York: Basic Books, 1977), pp. 16-18.
5. Ibid., p. 29.
6. Michael Warren, "Youth and Religious Nurture," in *Changing Patterns of Religious Education*, ed. Marvin J. Taylor (Nashville: Abingdon Press, 1984), p. 247.
7. Kett, *Rites of Passage*, p. 210.
8. Ibid., italics mine.
9. G. Stanley Hall, *Adolescence: Vol. I and Vol. II* (New York: Appleton, 1904).
10. August de B. Hollingshead, *Elmtown's Youth: The Impact of Social Class on Adolescents* (New York: Wiley, 1949), p. 149.
11. These conditions are detailed in a number of books; of interest here is Herbert G. Gutman, *The Black Family in Slavery and Freedom, 1750-1925* (New York: Pantheon Books, 1976).
12. Ibid., p. 3.
13. Ibid., p. 17.
14. Ibid., p. 75.
15. Joanne M. Martin and Elmer P. Martin, *The Helping Tradition in the Black Family and Community* (Silver Spring, Md.: National Association of Social Workers, 1985), p. 24.
16. Eugene D. Genovese, *Roll, Jordan Roll: The World the Slaves Made* (New York: Pantheon Books, 1974), p. 510.
17. Gutman, *Black Family*, p. 17.
18. Gary B. Nash, *Red, White, and Black: The Peoples of Early America* (Englewood Cliffs, N.J.: Prentice-Hall, 1974), p. 192.
19. Gutman, *Black Family*, p. 402.
20. Reynolds Farley, *Blacks and Whites, Narrowing the Gap?* (Cambridge: Harvard University Press, 1984), p. 203.
21. Martin and Martin, *Helping Tradition*, p. 59.
22. Gutman, *Black Family*, p. 466.
23. *The Chicago Tribune*, March 12, 1989, section 1, p.3.
24. Could this be a switch from Stage 3 to Stage 4 in James Fowler's schema? *Stages of Faith: The Psychology of Human Development and the Quest for Meaning* (San Francisco: Harper & Row, 1981).

25. Both Charles Marx and Michael Smathers are ordained Presbyterian (U.S.A.) ministers.
26. See Philip Phenix, "Transcendence and the Curriculum," in *Conflicting Conceptions of Curriculum*, eds. Elliot W. Eisner and Elizabeth Vallance (Berkeley: Stanford University Press, 1974), pp. 117-35.
27. See especially Paulo Freire, *Pedagogy of the Oppressed* (New York: Seabury Press, ninth printing, 1973).
28. We met in Martin Luther King Jr.'s old frame house. King had turned this building into his Atlanta training center. We slept on the floor and in the backyard.
29. James Bell, an ordained Presbyterian (U.S.A.) pastor.
30. Later that summer, SCLC led a strong series of demonstrations, centered on educational reform in Hope's county.
31. This was Hiland Presbyterian Church in the North Hills/West View area of Pittsburgh. William McKee Aber was the minister.
32. *Theological Themes of Youth Ministry* (New York: Pilgrim Press, 1987).
33. See especially Janice E. Hale-Benson, *Black Children: Their Roots, Culture, and Learning Styles* (Baltimore: Johns Hopkins University Press, 1988), and Thomas Kochman, *Black and White Styles in Conflict* (Chicago: University of Chicago Press, 1981).
34. Gayraud S. Wilmore, *Black and Presbyterian: The Heritage and the Hope* (Philadelphia: Geneva Press, 1983), p. 39, italics mine.
35. Kochman, *Black and White Styles*, p. 18.
36. Ibid., p. 19.
37. Ibid., p. 21.
38. Ibid., pp. 29-30.
39. James M. Gustafson, *Christian Ethics and the Community* (Philadelphia: Pilgrim Press, 1971), p. 180.
40. Ibid., see pp. 180-82.
41. Ibid., p. 184.
42. Henry H. Mitchell, "Black Preaching," in *Black Church Life-Styles*, ed. Emmanuel L. McCall (Nashville: Broadman Press, 1986), p. 109.
43. Gustafson, *Christian Ethics*, p. 184.
44. Among the presentations: "Educational Models for Youth: Black and White Contexts," a research paper presented at the biannual conference of the Society for Research in Child Development, Baltimore, 1987; "A Case Study of Grace Church: A Black Youth Ministry Program," research paper presented at the Association of Professors and Researchers in Religious Education, Washington, D.C., 1986; "A Case Study of St. Andrew's: A White Youth Ministry Program," research paper presented at the Association of Professors and Researchers in Religious Education, Chicago, 1985.

45. Walter Brueggemann, "Teaching as Witness," in *The Pastor as Teacher*, eds. Earl E. Shelp and Ronald H. Sunderland (New York: Pilgrim Press, 1989).

46. Ibid., p. 57.

47. Ibid., p. 58. See Robert H. Bellah et al., *Habits of the Heart: Individualism and Commitment in American Life* (Berkeley and Los Angeles: University of California Press, 1985); Crawford McPherson, *The Political Theory of Possessive Individualism: Hobbes to Locke* (Oxford: Clarendon Press, 1962); and Alasdair MacIntyre, *After Virtue: A Study in Moral Theory* (Notre Dame: University of Notre Dame Press, 1984).

48. R.E. Stake, "The Case Study Method in Social Inquiry," *Educational Researcher*, vol.7, no. 2 (1978), p. 7.

Chapter 4

1. Excerpted from Leonard Freeman's interview with Robert Bellah regarding the publication of *Habits of the Heart* (Los Angeles: University of California Press, 1985) with Richard Madsen, William M. Sullivan, Ann Swidler, and Steven M. Tipton. The interview was for the *Searching* television series and was initially printed in "Trinity News," vol. 33:3, New York: *Trinity Parish Newsletter*, August 1986.

2. See Erik Erikson, *Identity, Youth and Crisis* (New York: Norton, 1968), pp. 91-142 passim.

3. See Robert L. Moore, "Space and Transformation in Human Experience," in *Anthropology and the Study of Religion*, eds. Robert L. Moore and Frank E. Reynolds (Center for the Scientific Study of Religion, 5757 S. University Ave., Chicago, Ill. 60637), pp. 136ff.

4. Steve Jones, *Faith Shaping: Youth and the Experience of Faith* (Valley Forge: Judson Press, 1987), pp. 20-21.

5. Craig Dykstra, "Agenda for Youth Ministry: Problems, Questions, and Strategies," in *Readings and Resources in Youth Ministry*, ed. Michael Warren (Winona, Minn.: St. Mary's Press, 1987), p. 81.

6. See James Gustafson, *Treasure in Earthen Vessels: The Church as a Human Community* (New York: Harper & Row, 1961).

7. Ibid., pp. 10-11.

8. Ibid., p. 44.

9. Michael Warren, *Youth, Gospel, Liberation* (San Francisco: Harper & Row, 1987), p. ix.

10. Martin E. Marty, "Reformed America and America Reformed." *The Reformed Journal*, vol. 39, issue 3 (March 1989), p. 10.

11. David M. Scheider and Raymond T. Smith, "Class Differences and Sex Roles in American Kinship and Family Structure," in *Individualism*

and *Commitment in American Life: Readings on the Themes of Habits of the Heart*, eds. Robert N. Bellah, William M. Sullivan, Ann Swidler, and Steven M. Tipton (New York: Harper & Row, 1987), pp. 218-19.

12. Arthur G. Powell, Eleanor Farrar, and David K. Cotten, *The Shopping Mall High School: Winners and Losers in the Educational Marketplace* (Boston: Houghton Mifflin, 1985), p. 3.

13. Ibid.

14. Ibid.

15. Stanley K. Schultz, *The Culture Factory: Boston Public Schools, 1789-1860* (New York: Oxford University Press, 1973), p. 29.

16. Ibid.

17. Charles Leslie Glenn, Jr., *The Myth of the Common School* (Amherst: University of Massachusetts Press, 1988), p. 74.

18. Ibid., p. 236.

19. Ibid., p. 88.

20. Ibid., p. 227-29.

21. Ibid., p. 235.

22. Ibid., p. 139.

23. Ibid., p. 178.

24. Clarence J. Karier, *Shaping the American Educational State: 1900 to the Present* (New York: Free Press, Macmillan, 1975), p. xix.

25. Ibid., p. 2.

26. Ibid.

27. Robert N. Bellah, Richard Madsen, William M. Sullivan, Ann Swidler, Steven M. Tipton, *Habits of the Heart: Individualism and Commitment in American Life* (Los Angeles: University of California Press, 1985), p. 120.

28. Burton Bledstein, "The Culture of Professionalism," in *Individualism and Commitment in American Life*, p. 294.

29. Louis B. Weeks, "The 'Incorporation' of the Presbyterians," in *Reformanda* (Louisville: Louisville Theological Seminary, 1044 Alta Vista Road, 40205-1798), front and back pages.

30. Barbara G. Wheeler, "What Kind of Leadership for Tomorrow's Churches?" *Action Information*, vol. 9, no. 6 (Alban Institute, November/December, 1985), p. 10.

Chapter 5

1. Maria Harris, commenting on John Baptist Metz's idea of "dangerous listening." See Maria Harris, "Holy Place, Teaching Place," in *The Pastor as Teacher*, eds. Earl E. Shelp and Ronald H. Sunderland (New York: Pilgrim Press, 1989), p. 16; John Baptist Metz, *Faith in History and Society* (New York: Seabury Press, 1980), pp. 109-10.

2. E. Franklin Frazier, *The Negro Church in America* (New York: Schocken Books, 1963), p. 20.

3. Lerone Bennett Jr., *The Shaping of Black America* (Chicago: Johnson Publishing Co., 1975), p. 48.

4. Ibid., p. 46.

5. Ibid., p. 50.

6. Ibid., p. 41.

7. Ibid., p. 53.

8. Ibid., p. 45.

9. Joseph R. Washington Jr., *Black Religion: The Negro and Christianity in the United States* (Boston: Beacon Press, 1964), p. 165.

10. Frazier, *Negro Church*, p. 20.

11. Bennett, *Shaping*, p. 22.

12. Washington, *Black Religion*, p. 171. See footnote 8, same page.

13. James Oakes, *The Ruling Race: A History of American Slaveholders* (New York: Alfred A. Knopf, 1982), p. 11.

14. Eugene D. Genovese, *Roll, Jordan, Roll: The World the Slaves Made* (New York: Random House/Pantheon Books, 1974), p. 202.

15. Ibid., p. 203.

16. Washington, *Black Religion*, p. 166.

17. Bennett, *Shaping*, p. 67.

18. John Hope Franklin, *From Slavery to Freedom* (New York: Alfred A. Knopf, 1948), pp. 85-86.

19. Bennett, *Shaping*, p. 147.

20. Ibid., p. 147.

21. Ibid., p. 72.

22. Albert J. Raboteau, *Slave Religion: The "Invisible Institution" in the Antebellum South* (New York: Oxford University Press, 1978), p. 128.

23. Emmanuel L. McCall, "Black Baptist Church History," in *Black Church Life-Styles*, ed. Emmanuel L. McCall (Nashville: Broadman Press, 1986), p. 24.

24. Genovese, *Roll, Jordan*, p. 185.

25. Ibid.

26. Washington, *Black Religion*, p. 187.

27. Genovese, *Roll, Jordan*, p. 232.

28. Raboteau, *Slave Religion*, p. 131.

29. Ibid., p. 132.

30. Ibid., p. 134-39.

31. Genovese, *Roll, Jordan*, p. 185.

32. Lawrence Jones, "The Organized Church," in *Negotiating the Main Stream: A Survey of the Afro-American Experience*, ed. Harry A. Johnson (United States: American Library Association, 1978), p. 105.

33. Washington, *Black Religion*, p. 202.

34. Ibid., p. 187.
35. Bennett, *Shaping*, p. 29.
36. Genovese, *Roll, Jordan*, p. 184.
37. Ibid., p. 162.
38. Ibid.
39. Ibid., p. 210.
40. Ibid., p. 213.
41. Ibid.
42. Gayraud S. Wilmore, *Black and Presbyterian: The Heritage and the Hope* (Philadelphia: Geneva Press, 1983), p. 41.
43. Bennett, *Shaping*, p. 163.
44. Genovese, *Roll, Jordan*, pp. 233-34.
45. Ibid., p. 148.
46. Frazier, *Negro Church*, p. 31.
47. Raboteau, *Slave Religion*, p. 290.
48. Ibid., p. 296.
49. Genovese, *Roll, Jordan*, p. 186.
50. Ibid., p. 188.
51. Ibid.
52. Ibid., p. 189.
53. Ibid., p. 188.
54. Ibid., p. 187.
55. John R. McKivigan, *The War against Proslavery Religion: Abolitionism and the Northern Churches, 1830-1865* (Ithaca: Cornell University Press, 1984), pp. 14-16.
56. Ibid., pp. 13-14.
57. Ibid., p. 7.
58. Ibid., p. 14.
59. Ibid., p. 16.
60. Genovese, *Roll, Jordan*, p. 235.
61. Jones, "Organized Church," pp. 106-7. For Jones's footnote 12, see Donald J. Matthews, *Slavery and Methodism* (Princeton: Princeton University Press, 1965), pp. 64-65.
62. Jones, "Organized Church," p. 107.
63. Washington, *Black Religion*, p. 188.
64. Frazier, *Negro Church*, p. 27.
65. Washington, *Black Religion*, p. 188.
66. Ibid., p. 189.
67. Bennet, *Shaping*, p. 126.
68. Jones, "Organized Church," p. 117.
69. Ibid., p. 116.
70. Ibid., pp. 116-17.

Chapter 6

1. Wallace Charles Smith, *The Church in the Life of the Black Family* (Valley Forge: Judson Press, 1985), p. 60.
2. Ibid., p. 22.
3. Ibid.
4. Ibid.
5. Ibid., p. 61.
6. Herbert G. Gutman, *The Black Family in Slavery and Freedom, 1750-1925* (New York: Pantheon Books, 1976), p. 217.
7. Marilyn M. White, "We are Family! Kinship and Solidarity in the Black Community," in *Expressively Black: The Cultural Basis of Ethnic Identity,* eds. Geneva Gay and Willie L. Barber (New York: Praeger, 1987), p. 18.
8. Gutman, *Black Family,* p. 230.
9. Joanne M. Martin and Elmer P. Martin, *The Helping Tradition in the Black Family and Community* (Silver Spring, Md.: National Association of Social Workers, 1985), p. 18.
10. Gutman, *Black Family,* p. 222.
11. Ibid., pp. 226ff.
12. Ibid., p. 229.
13. Joseph R. Washington Jr., *Black Religion* (Boston: Beacon Press, 1964), p. 34.
14. Martin and Martin, *Helping Tradition,* pp. 61ff.
15. Ibid., p. 65.
16. E. Franklin Frazier, *The Negro Church in America* (New York: Schocken Books, 1963), p. 14.
17. James P. Comer, *Beyond Black and White* (New York: Quadrangle Books, 1972), p. 18.
18. Ibid.
19. Frazier, *Negro Church,* p. 45.
20. Comer, *Beyond Black,* p. 16.
21. Washington, *Black Religion,* p. 37.
22. Ibid., p. 225.
23. Martin and Martin, *Helping Tradition,* p. 63.
24. Ibid., p. 69.
25. Elmer P. Martin and Joanne Mitchell Martin, *The Black Extended Family* (Chicago: University of Chicago Press, 1978), pp. 101-2.
26. Martin and Martin, *Helping Tradition,* p. 67.
27. Romney M. Moseley, "Retrieving Intergenerational and Intercultural Faith for Black Youth," a paper prepared for a consultation on ministries to black youth sponsored by the Lilly Endowment Project on Youth Ministry (Scarritt Graduate School, Nashville, November 5-7, 1987), p. 15.

28. Bart Landry, *The New Black Middle Class* (Berkeley: University of California Press, 1987), p. 3.

29. Ibid., p. 75.

30. Ibid., p. 92, italics mine.

31. Ibid., p. 94.

32. Richard Lacayo, "Between Two Worlds." *Time*, vol. 133, no. 11 (March 3, 1989), p. 58.

33. Nancy Denton and Douglas Massey, *The University of Chicago Magazine* (Spring 1989), p. 37.

34. Ibid., p. 38.

35. James E. Ellis, "The Black Middle Class: After Years of Hard-Won Progress, Signs of Stagnation are Appearing." *Business Week* (March 14, 1988), p. 69.

36. James Lardner, "Rich, Richer; Poor, Poorer," *The New York Times*, Wednesday, April 19, 1989, p. 23.

37. Ibid.

38. Martin and Martin, *Helping Tradition*, p. 68.

39. Ibid., p. 71.

40. Ibid., p. 73.

41. Ibid., p. 74.

42. Geneva Gay, "Ethnic Identity Development and Black Expressiveness," in *Expressively Black: The Cultural Basis of Ethnic Identity*, eds. Geneva Gay and Willie L. Barber (New York: Praeger, 1987), p. 37.

43. Ibid., p. 64.

44. Ibid., p. 42.

45. Ibid., p. 66.

Chapter 8

1. Stephen D. Jones, *Faith Shaping: Nurturing the Faith Journey of Youth* (Valley Forge: Judson Press, 1980), p. 8.

2. Ibid., p. 24.

3. Ibid., p. 30.

4. Ibid., p. 32.

Chapter 9

1. Maria Harris, *Fashion Me a People: Curriculum in the Church* (Louisville: Westminster/John Knox Press, 1989), p. 16.

2. Charles R. Foster, "Abundance of Managers ... Scarcity of Teachers." *Religious Education*, vol. 80 (Summer 1985), p. 441.

3. Ibid., p. 439, italics mine.

4. Ibid., p. 438, italics mine.

5. Frank T. Fair, *ORITA* for *Black Youth: An Initiation into Christian Adulthood* (Valley Forge: Judson Press, 1977).

Chapter 10

1. Songwriter Sam Phillips, quoted in Nancy Stetson, "Indescribable Wow," *Chicago Tribune Tempo Section*, section 5 (Wednesday, April 19, 1989), p. 3.
2. James Gustafson, *Treasure in Earthen Vessels: The Church as a Human Community* (New York: Harper & Row, 1961), p. 11.
3. See Philip Greven, *The Protestant Temperament: Patterns of Child-Rearing, Religious Experience, and the Self in Early America* (New York: New American Library, 1977).
4. See Martin E. Marty, "Reformed America and America Reformed." *The Reformed Journal*, vol. 39, issue 3 (March 1989), p. 8.
5. Charles R. Foster, "The Anglo Religious Education Experience," in *Ethnicity in the Education of the Church*, ed. Charles R. Foster (Nashville: Scarritt Press, 1987), p. 60.
6. Ibid., pp. 61-62.
7. Ibid., p. 62.
8. See John H. Westerhoff, *Will Our Children Have Faith?* (New York: Seabury Press, 1976); also Maria Harris, *Fashion Me a People: Curriculum in the Church* (Louisville: Westminster/John Knox, 1989).
9. Check John Snow, *The Impossible Vocation* (Cambridge, Mass.: Cowley Publications, 1988); and Merle R. Jordan, *Taking on the Gods: The Task of the Pastoral Counselor* (Nashville: Abingdon Press, 1986), on the growing concern regarding metaphors from management and therapy in the church.
10. Ella Mitchell, "Black Nurture," in *Black Church LifeStyles*, ed. Emmanuel McCall (Nashville: Broadman Press, 1986), p. 64.
11. Ibid., p. 45.
12. Ibid., p. 47.
13. Ibid., p. 49.
14. Ibid., pp. 53-54.
15. Ibid., pp. 55-56.
16. H. Shelton Smith, *Faith and Nurture* (New York: Charles Scribner's Sons, 1950; original edition, 1941), cover; italics mine.
17. Ibid., pp. 4-26.
18. Ibid., p. 56.
19. Ibid., p. 30.
20. Ibid., p. 60.
21. Robert N. Bellah, Richard Madsen, William M. Sullivan, Ann Swidler, and Steven M. Tipton, *Habits of the Heart* (Berkeley: University of California Press, 1985).

22. Vic Jameson, "Civil Religion: An Interview with Isabel Rogers." *Presbyterian Survey* (Jan.-Feb. 1988), p. 15.

23. James P. Comer, *Beyond Black and White* (New York: Quadrangle Books, 1972), p. 78.

24. Bellah, et. al., *Habits of the Heart*, pp. 44-45.

25. Robert N. Bellah, "Introduction," in *Individualism and Commitment in American Life: Readings on the Themes of Habits of the Heart*, eds. Robert N. Bellah, Richard Madsen, William M. Sullivan, Ann Swidler, and Steven M. Tipton (New York: Harper & Row, 1987), p. 8.

26. Gustafson, *Treasure*, p. 44.

27. Ibid., p. 51.

28. Ibid.

29. James M. Gustafson, *The Church as Moral Decision-Maker* (Philadelphia: Pilgrim Press, 1970), p. 86.

30. Ibid., p. 89.

31. Ibid., pp. 60-61.

32. Janice E. Hale-Benson, *Black Children: Their Roots, Culture, and Learning Styles* (Baltimore: Johns Hopkins University Press, 1986), p. 5.

33. Ibid., p. 34.

34. Ibid., p. 187, italics mine.

35. Foster, "Anglo Experience," p. 59.

36. Dorothy C. Bass, "Teaching with Authority? The Changing Place of Mainstream Protestantism in American Culture," in *Mainstream Protestantism in the Twentieth Century: Its Problems and Prospects,* papers presented to the 1986 annual meeting of the Council of Theological Education, Presbyterian Church (U.S.A.), p. 8.

37. Amos Jones, Jr., "Response," in *Ethnicity in the Education of the Church*, ed. Charles R. Foster (Nashville: Scarritt Press, 1987), p. 71.

38. Ibid., p. 72.

39. Williams R. Myers, "The Church in the World: Models of Youth Ministry." *Theology Today*, vol. 44 (April 1987), pp. 103-10.

40. Consider, for example, the "spiritual" model of David J. Stone, *Spiritual Growth in Youth Ministry* (Loveland, Colo.: Group Books, 1985); the "team" model of Ginny Ward Holderness, *Youth Ministry: The New Team Model* (Atlanta: John Knox Press, 1981); the "congregational" model of Stephen S. Jones, *Faith Shaping: Nurturing the Faith Journey of Youth* (Valley Forge: Judson Press, 1980); and the "peer ministry" model of Brian Reynolds, *A Chance to Serve: A Leader's Manual for Peer Ministry* (Winona, Minn.: Saint Mary's Press, 1984).

41. Paulo Freire, *Pedagogy of the Oppressed* (New York: Seabury Press, 1973, ninth printing), p. 30.

42. William R. Myers, "Models for Urban Youth Ministry: Goals, Styles, and Contexts," in *Urban Church Education*, ed. Donald B. Rogers (Birmingham: Religious Education Press, 1989), pp. 130-131.

43. See Stephen S. Jones, *Faith Shaping: Nurturing the Faith Journey of Youth* (Valley Forge: Judson Press, 1980), pp. 24-30.

44. H. Richard Niebuhr, *Christ and Culture* (New York: Harper & Brothers, 1951).

45. David A. Roozen, William McKinney, and Jackson W. Carroll, *Varieties of Religious Presence* (New York: Pilgrim Press, 1984).

46. Charles R. Foster, "Abundance of Managers, Scarcity of Teachers." *Religious Education*, vol. 80 (1985), p. 438.